The Great Dobro®

MW00666958

transcribed & annotated by Stacy Phillips
(with Curtis Burch & Mike Auldridge)

A Gathering of Resophonic Pickers

Mike Auldridge, Curtis Burch, Jerry Douglas, Josh Graves, Rob Ickes, Oswald Kirby, Stacy Phillips, Tut Taylor, Sally Van Meter, Gene Wooten

A recording of the music in this book is now available. The publisher strongly recommends the use of this recording along with the text to ensure accuracy of interpretation and ease in learning.

"DOBRO" is a registered trademark owned by Original Musical Instrument Company, a division of Gibson Guitar Corporation. "DOBRO" refers to a particular brand of guitar. The generic name for this style of guitar playing is "resonator guitar" or "resophonic guitar."

MEL BAY ®

SUGAR HILL

Published in conjunction with Sugar Hill Records.

Visit us on the Web at http://www.melbay.com — E-mail us at email@melbay.com

Contents

ACKNOWLEDGMENTS

Curtis Burch for transcribing the second half of "Little Green Pill #2" and all of "Suitcase" and "Rainbow Bridge."

Mike Auldridge for the eight-string version of "Wave."

Introduction

It is as if it happened yesterday. A gray New England afternoon shaded into the dark abyss of night. The jangling phone woke me from my reverie. "Hi Stacy, this is Jerry. Come on down to Nashville. We're getting all the DOBRO® pickers together to record," the voice drawled. "I'll be right down," I mumbled as I crammed some clothes into a satchel. "By the way, Jerry who?" So began my adventures in The Southland with *The Great DOBRO® Sessions* album.

On the flight down the attendant turned out to be a country song writer who hired me for some overdubbing on his own project after I recorded my two tunes for the album. He ignored the frantic signals of famished passengers to yodel a few choruses of one of his compositions for me. It happens on every airplane to Music City, USA.

I was lodged at a motel in downtown Nashville. In what I imagine was a typical welcome to town, as I entered the adjoining restaurant, a patron was being wheeled out on a stretcher to a waiting ambulance. Inside the patrons were gumming grits as if nothing had happened. I kept my mouth shut and my hand on my wallet. Outside the streets smelled of hair spray and Dentyne™ chewing gum by day as bee hive hairdos and drug store cowboys roamed freely through the casbah of souvenirs. By night the streets emptied, leaving a few guitar-picking nighthawks searching the city lights for the elusive jam session that would make their reputation. I shivered as the glow of neon signs reflected off of a sad pool of discarded spangles and sequins entangled in wads of used gum and empty hair mousse containers in the gutter. The name is Phillips. I play a resophonic steel guitar.

On the evening before the sessions began we gathered at the studio. It was sweet to have the whole gaggle of resonator guitarists in one room if only for a few hours. No doubt the unprecedented high density of lap slides triggered klaxons in the underground bunkers of the music police. The critical mass of spun and stamped resonators was almost reached and a tragic meltdown narrowly avoided by allowing each of us generous personal space in the studio.

Two players per day were recorded but most of us were in and out during the rest of the week to check out and support each other's efforts, as well as to nudge Tut awake. (Tut was a main driving force in bringing this album concept to fruition.) Meanwhile wolf packs of acoustic music's best musicians swirled in and prowled about, waiting to accompany the next resophonic artiste.

With the help of producers Jerry Douglas and Tut Taylor, and engineer Bill Vorn Dick, *The Great DOBRO® Sessions* won a Grammy for best bluegrass album and IBMA awards for both best instrumental album and recorded event of the year.

****

A transcriber cannot help but be prejudiced towards hearing riffs the way he or she might play them. The resonator steel guitar is a difficult instrument to transcribe for several reasons. For one, it blends in well with other instruments making it hard to hear clearly in detail. Secondly the choice of fret and string is critical to personal style but difficult to discern. Additionally there are all sorts of un-notateable parameters of slurs, tricky damping and note overlaps, etc. I plead guilty to occasionally using my febrile imagination when the solos got hot. You might try asking the artists what they actually played next time you see them. Otherwise, experiment with different string and fret combinations for any musical phrase you like. The one that is easiest for you should be your choice. I sometimes decided the way that I would fret a lick, then discarded that option as the least likely that any of these great players would choose. I had enough trouble trying to tab my own two entries. "Did I actually play that?"

We were unable to include Gene Wooten's fine rendition of "Day Tripper" because of corporate greed.

Curtis Burch transcribed his two pieces as well as the last solo of "Little Green Pill."

It was a pleasure to have a chance to sit down and carefully analyze the playing of some of the acoustic steel guitarists I have always admired. I thank William Bay of Mel Bay Publications for the chance.

This book is dedicated to John Dopyera Sr. of Slovakia and America, whose imagination, determination and superior artisanship made the resonator guitar a reality. I also wish to acknowledge the efforts of John Dopyera Jr. of Pennsylvania and Josef Dopjera (and his briefcase full of ideas) of Piestany, Slovakia for their efforts in making the DOBRO® Festival a reality.

Stacy Phillips
New Haven, Connecticut
February, 1996

Reading the Tablature

Written music notation is meant as a rough interpretation, not as a literal representation. There is too much going on to tab everything.

With all the syncopated sliding, droning rolls and dense notation of some of these pieces, the only way to really learn them is to listen carefully to the recording on the Sugar Hill-2206 album. Notating all the damping and note overlaps would make the music too dense to be readable. The exact length and speed of slides, variations of vibrato and dynamics, as well as tricky rhythmic shenanigans can only be approximated or ignored in the tablature. I also did not specifically notate when the bar was in slant position. It is usually obvious from the notes that are played. I often did not notate one string continuing to ring while a new one was picked. Again the reason was to avoid overcrowding. The bottom line is you learn best by listening and watching.

The droning notes of open string rolls are often difficult to decipher. When you come upon an open string-type roll filler (i.e. a riff marking time between while the melody is static), take my interpretation with a grain of salt. The same is true of what I call arpeggiated fills in the text. These entail picking on various strings on one fret to fill in space between the actual melody or variation.

Unless otherwise stated all the guitars are tuned to an open G chord, from the first string down: D-B-G-D-B-G.

Here is a quick course in reading tablature. Don't bother memorizing this stuff. Refer back here when you cannot decipher the record and my notation is unclear to you.

Each of the six lines of the tablature represents a string, with the thinnest, highest pitched string at the top and the thickest, lowest pitched string at the bottom of the staff. It is just like looking down at your guitar in playing position. A number on a line indicates the fret and string that should be played. So:

means that you should first pick the first string, third fret (abbreviated as S1-F3), then the first string open, then string 2, fret 10, then S1-F8/S2-F8 simultaneously and, finally S1-F5/S3-F4.

The same sort of stems, flags and beams from standard music notation are attached to the fret numbers to indicate how long each note should be held. The time signature or meter at the beginning of the examples tells you their beat structure. The bottom number of 4/4 time signature means that a quarter note is one beat long. For our purpose, a beat can be considered the length of time it takes to tap your foot, lift it, and lower it, just to the point that it hits the floor again. The top number tells you how many beats there are per measure. The 4/4 meter has four quarter notes per measure. The 3/4 meter has three quarter note beats per measure and, in this book, always indicates a waltz.

When you see: (Here the 'X" stands for any fret number)

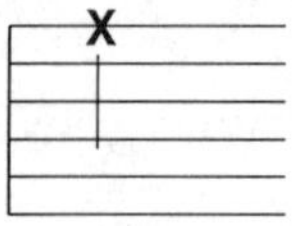

hold that note for the time it takes you to tap your foot once, from foot-on-floor until just before your foot taps again. The attached stem indicates one quarter note (and one beat if the denominator of the meter is 4, which it always is in this book). A circle around a fret number with a stem attached indicates a half note, held for two beats. A four-beat whole note is encircled but without a stem.

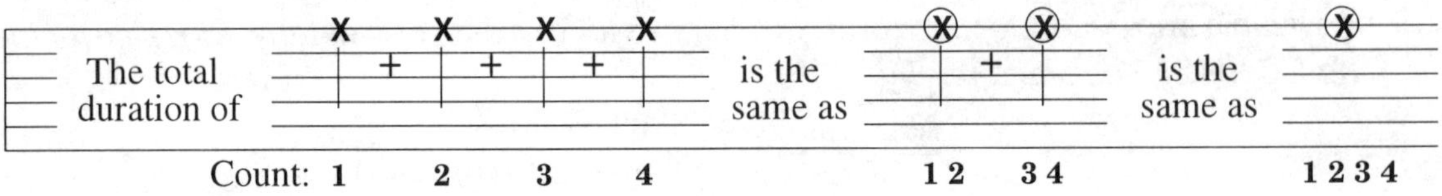

In the first grouping the note is picked four times; in the second, twice, with each note held twice as long; and, in the last, it is picked once. Whether the beam is up or down has no effect on the count.

A quarter note can be divided into two eighth notes, one when the foot is on the floor (sometimes called a strong beat) and the other when the foot is in the air. The latter is called the offbeat, upbeat or just "and." Beams and flags are attached to the stems to indicate durations shorter than a quarter note. When there is a consecutive series of short notes the flags are usually joined to form a beam.

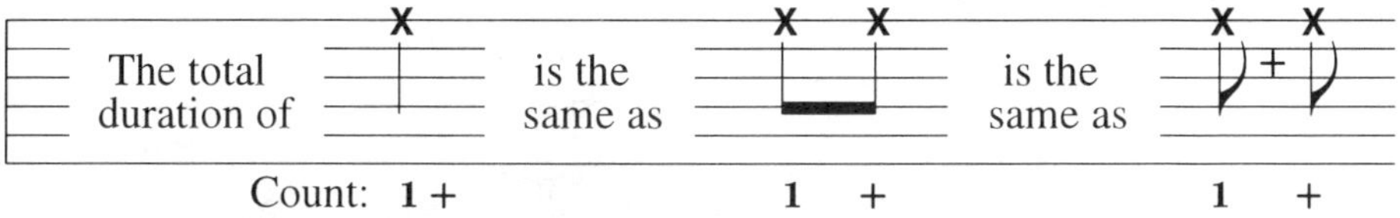

Eighths can be divided into sixteenths, symbolized by a second flag or beam.

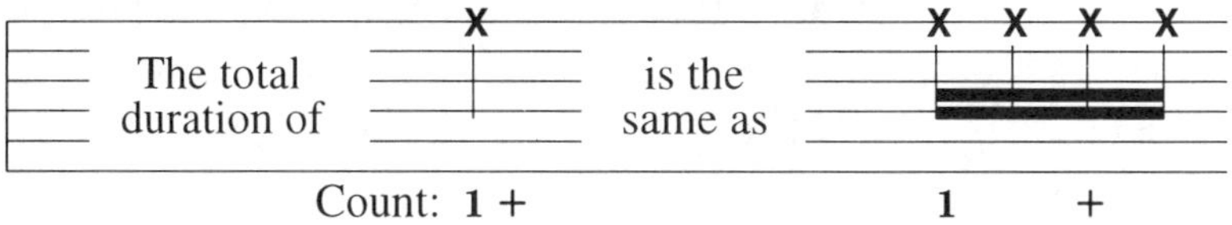

When a note is dotted, lengthen its duration by half its original value.

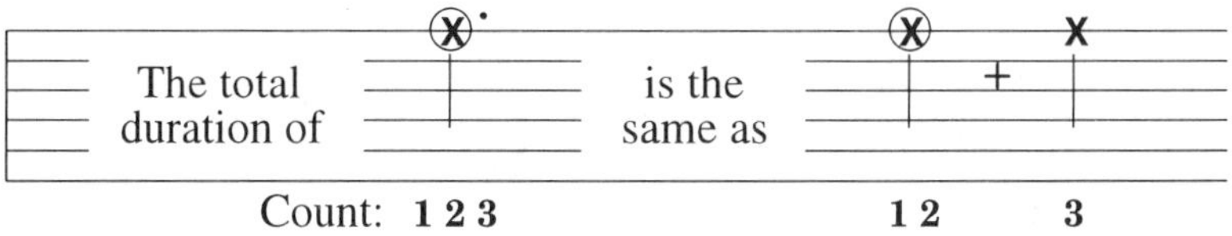

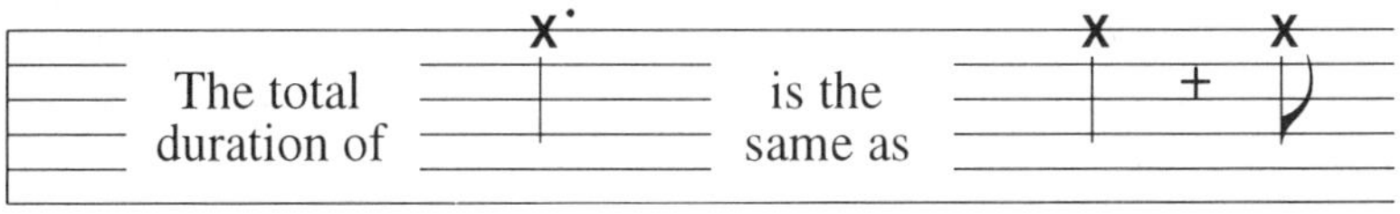

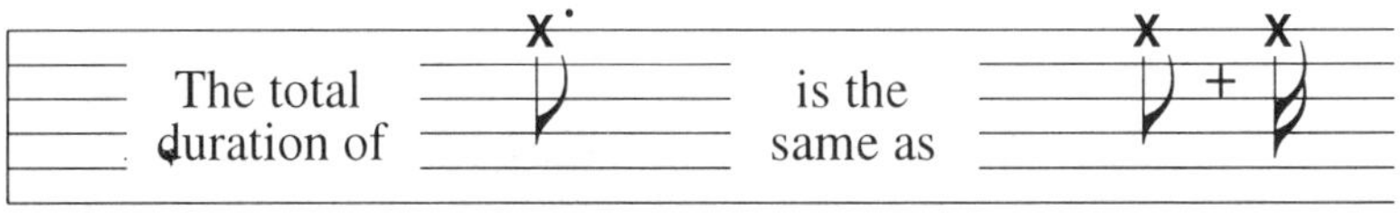

A second dot adds an additional quarter of the note's original value.

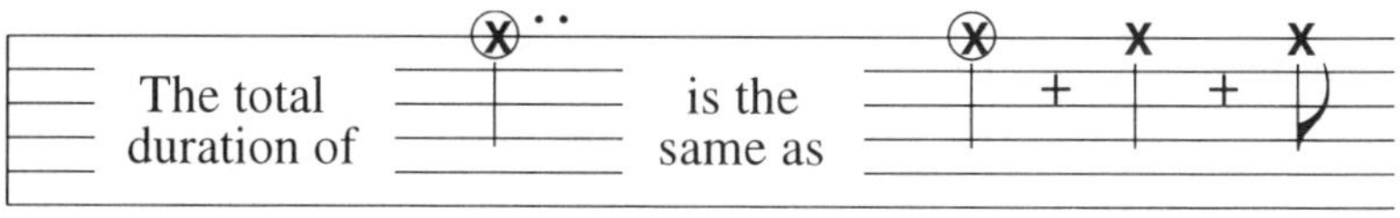

A quarter note triplet has its three notes evenly spaced within one beat. The first note is played on the strong beat; the second, just before the upbeat; and the third, just after.

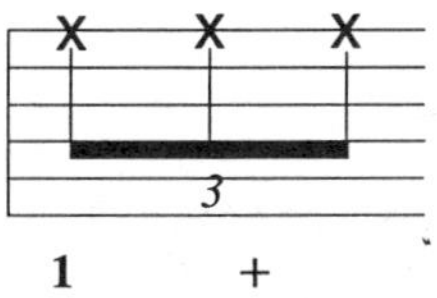

The eighth note triplet sounds three notes in the space of an eighth note (a half beat), and the half note triplet divides two beats into three equal durations.

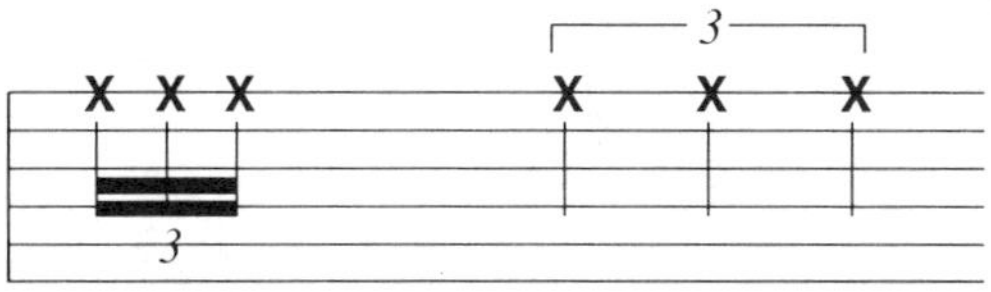

Rests have their own symbols but are counted similarly.

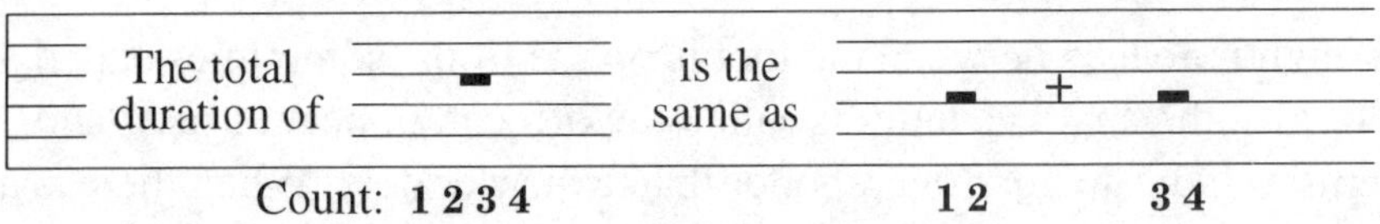

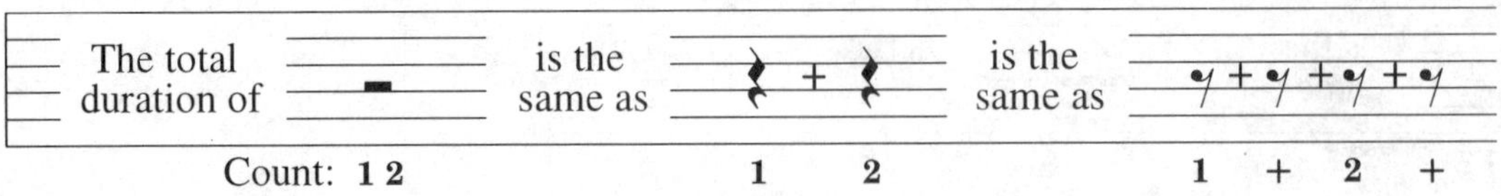

I use cut time meter - ¢ - as a device to eliminate relatively difficult to read passages on up tempo tunes that contain many sixteenth notes. This meter always has four quarter notes per measure, so it looks just like 4/4 time. For this book's purpose ¢ doubles the duration of each note and rest. So while being easier to read, the relative durations remain the same. You might wish to tap your foot twice as fast. For example, a measure with 2 quarter note beats per measure would be changed in the following manner.

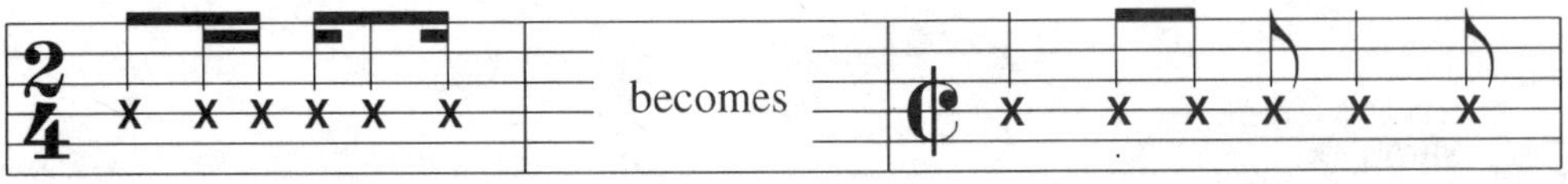

The abbreviation for strings and frets, e.g. "S3-F4" should be read, "third string, fourth fret." S1-F10/S3-F9 indicates that the bar should touch both the first string at the tenth fret and the third string at the ninth.

Hammer-ons and pull-offs have not been notated because of the difficulty of clearly hearing them amid the playing of the accompanying instruments. (Curtis Burch did tab a few in the tunes he transcribed.)

A curved slur sign indicates a continuous slide between the indicated notes. So

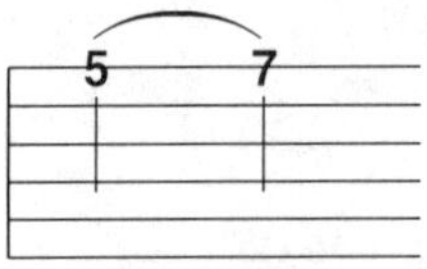

means to hold S1-F5 for a quarter note then quickly slide to the next note without picking.

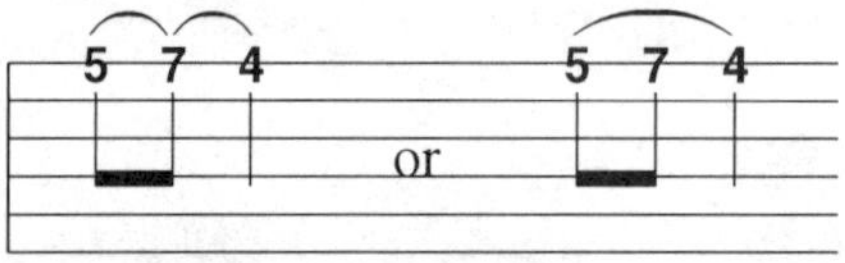

means to pick the first note only and slide to the others after holding each for the specified duration. When a legato symbol is used in conjunction with a slide:

it means to play as in the previous example but pick the second note when you arrive.

The same slur sign is used to extend the duration of a note when it crosses a bar line or the middle of a measure.

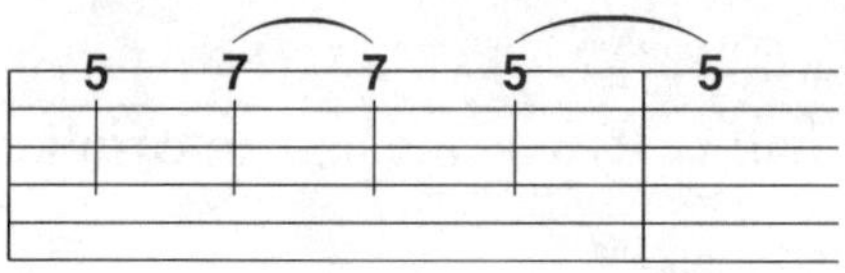

In these cases the symbol is referred to as a tie sign. In the above illustration S1-F7 is held through beats 2 and 3, and S1-F5 is held from beat 4 up to beat 2 of the next measure.
When the slur sign is not attached to a second note it means to let the first note ring. This is used to avoid overcrowded notation and is clear in context.

Diagonal lines attached to a note refer to (usually quick) slides of indeterminate length (usually one or less frets).

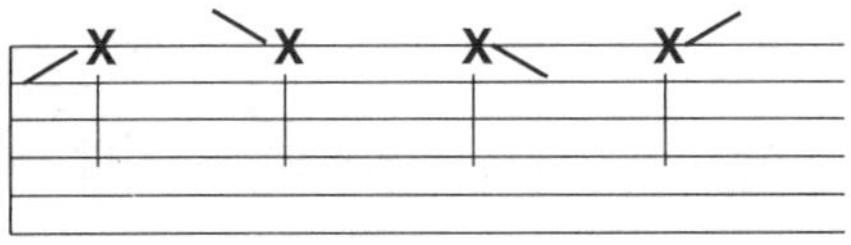

The direction of the lines indicates the direction of the slide. The first is up to; the next down to. The third is down from and the last is up from. Whether the beginning of the slide actually has no duration can be a subjective interpretation.

An arrow -↑- placed to the right of a note means you should "choke" (i.e. pull) the indicated string behind the bar so that its pitch is raised a half-step (i.e. one fret). So "5 ↑" means that, though the bar is on the 5th fret, the string is raised in pitch to the sound of the 6th fret.

↑↑ placed to the right of a note means that you should choke it a whole step (i.e. 2 frets worth). So "5 ↑↑" means that the bar is on the 5th fret and the note sounds as if it were on the 7th.

* placed to the right of a note means that the note is choked in pitch **up to** the indicated fret. This symbol occurs only in conjunction with slanted bar positions. So:

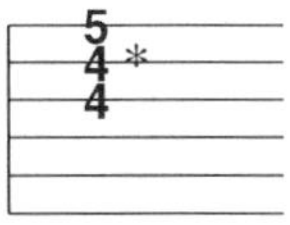

means that when the bar is place correctly on the first and third strings, it touches the second string midway between frets 4 and 5. That string is choked until the second string sounds the pitch of the fifth fret.

A vertical arrow *above* a note means it is played slightly sharp, on purpose.

The grace note above is held for the shortest possible time. What little time is usually taken from the previous beat, though it is a matter of personal taste whether to take it from the following note.

TR means tremolo, a rapid alternate picking of, usually, two adjacent strings.

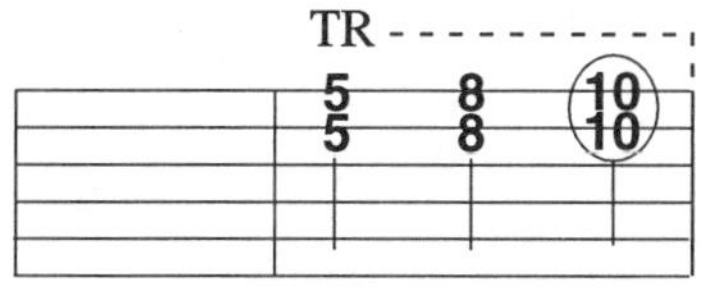

means to tremolo all the notes enclosed by the dashed line. If there is no dashed line just play it on the notes immediately under the symbol. There are a couple of unusual tremolos that are explained in the text. See "Flatt Lonesome" and "Lonesome DOBRO®."

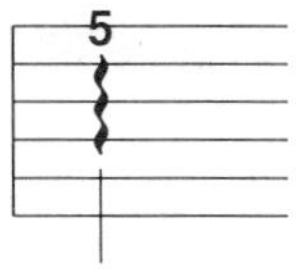

means to strum the strings as in a chord at the indicated fret. This indicates a C chord for one beat.

When the strum sign has an "x" on the string below the fret number it indicates a scrape or rip, i.e. a damped, accented strum except for the top string. It will be described in more detail later.

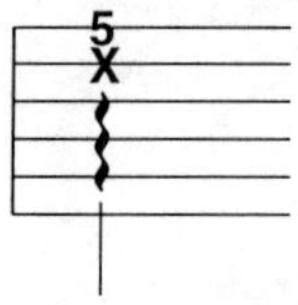

A staccato symbol placed over a note means to damp the sound and leave an audible space between the notes.

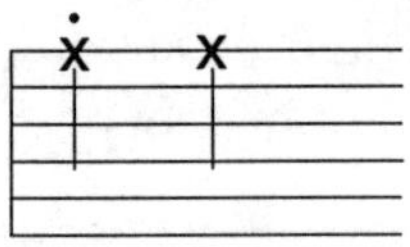

The actual timing might be:

° placed over a fret number indicates natural harmonics.

The following symbol over a particular fret number means to accent that note:

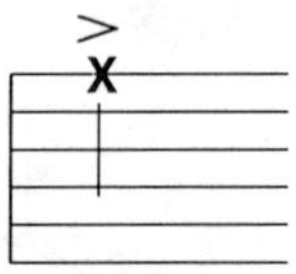

( ) Parentheses around a note mean one of two things, made clear in context.

a) a ghost note, i.e. a note at least partially damped, so the sound is there without any particular pitch.
b) the pitch at the beginning or end of a slide, or at a particular passing point in a long slide, when that pitch is given no duration.

Capital letters above the tablature indicate the chordal accompaniment.

Measure numbers are placed below and at the beginning of the staff.

The occasional numbers in a box indicate the different sections of a piece.

FIREBALL MAIL

by **Floyd Jenkins**

Nine of us got a shot at this one. Jerry assures me that this is the correct identity of the soloists. I used Mike's Ivan Guernsey guitar on this so I couldn't even identify my own playing.

Oswald recorded "Fireball Mail" with Roy Acuff in the 1940s, and Buck did it as an instrumental with Flatt and Scruggs about twenty years later. The rest of us owe much of our awareness of and love for resonator lap guitar to inspiration from those two fellows.

Buck kicks off with two passes, then we took one apiece. As will be true with most of the up-tempo tunes in this book, the exact components of the banjo-y, rolling fills often escaped me. Most of the solos on this piece are filled with them. However I am certain that my interpretations are reasonably close. You have to search a bit to find the melody notes among the welter of rolls.

The symbol in measure 25 implies one of Buck's signature moves, a scrape or rip damping the lower string while hitting the first string real strong. (See the Reading the Tablature chapter.)

The bracketed lick during Gene Wooten's solo was slid by one of the other guitarists. There are a couple of other instances of this scattered through this piece which I did not notate. The downward arrow in Jerry Douglas' solo indicates that he did not quite reach the indicated fret.

At the studio the night before the first session. Seated clockwise from the left: Mike Auldridge, Jerry Douglas, Tut Taylor (partially obscured), Buck Graves, Stacy Phillips, Pete Kirby. Standing from left: Rod Ickes, Gene Wooten, Curtis Burch. (Photo: Bill Vorn Dick.)

FIREBALL MAIL

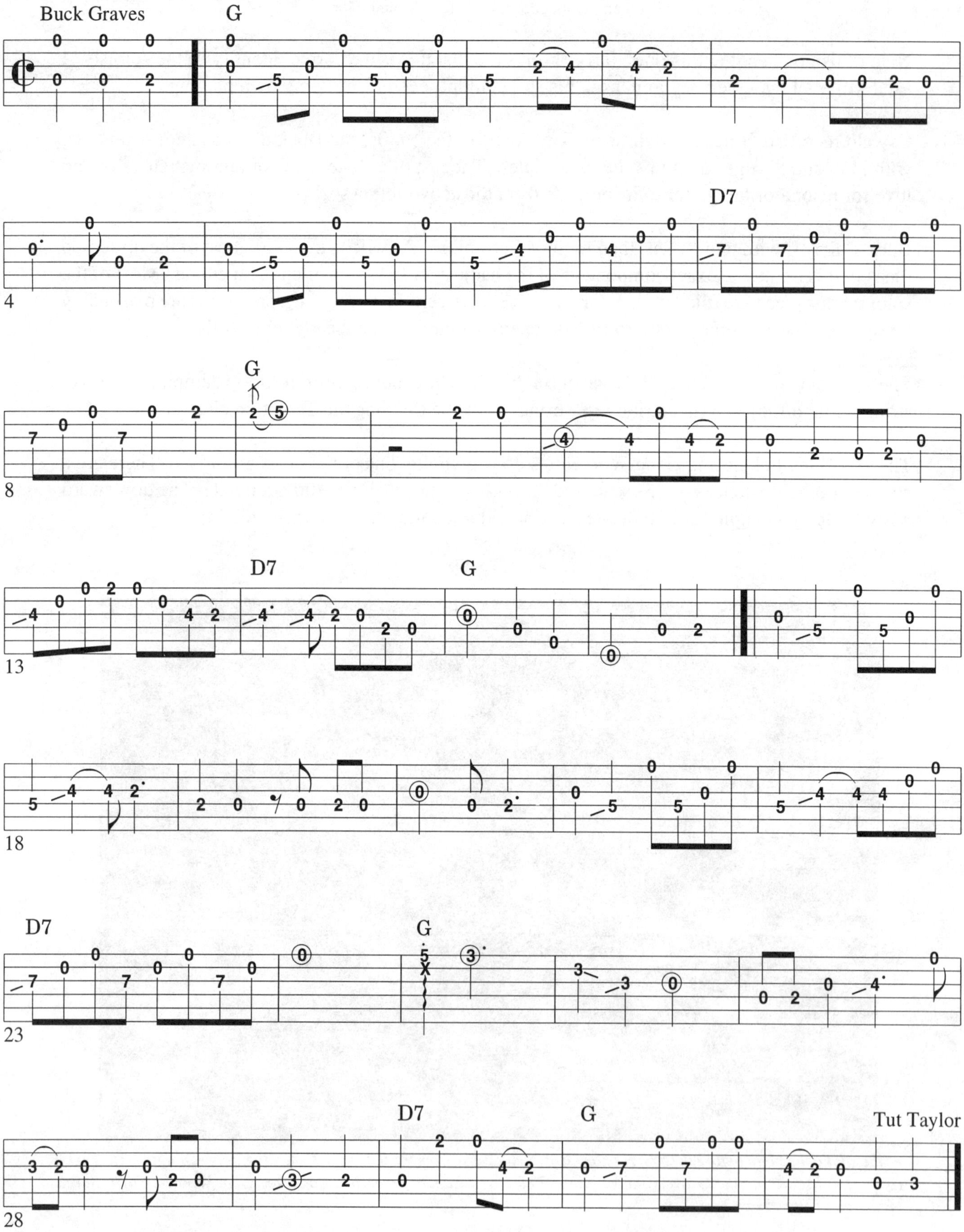

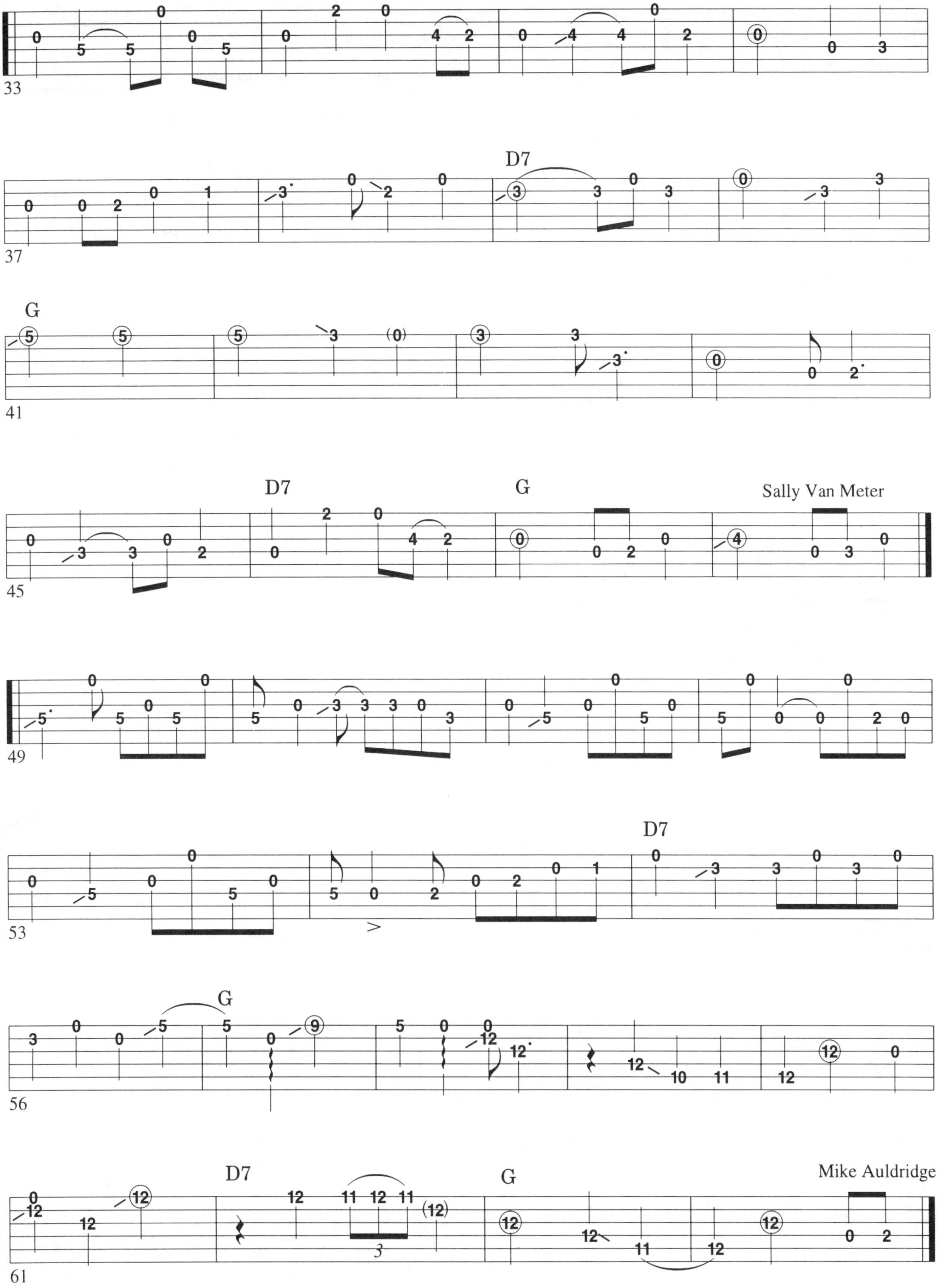
D7
G
D7
G
Sally Van Meter
D7
G
D7
G
Mike Auldridge

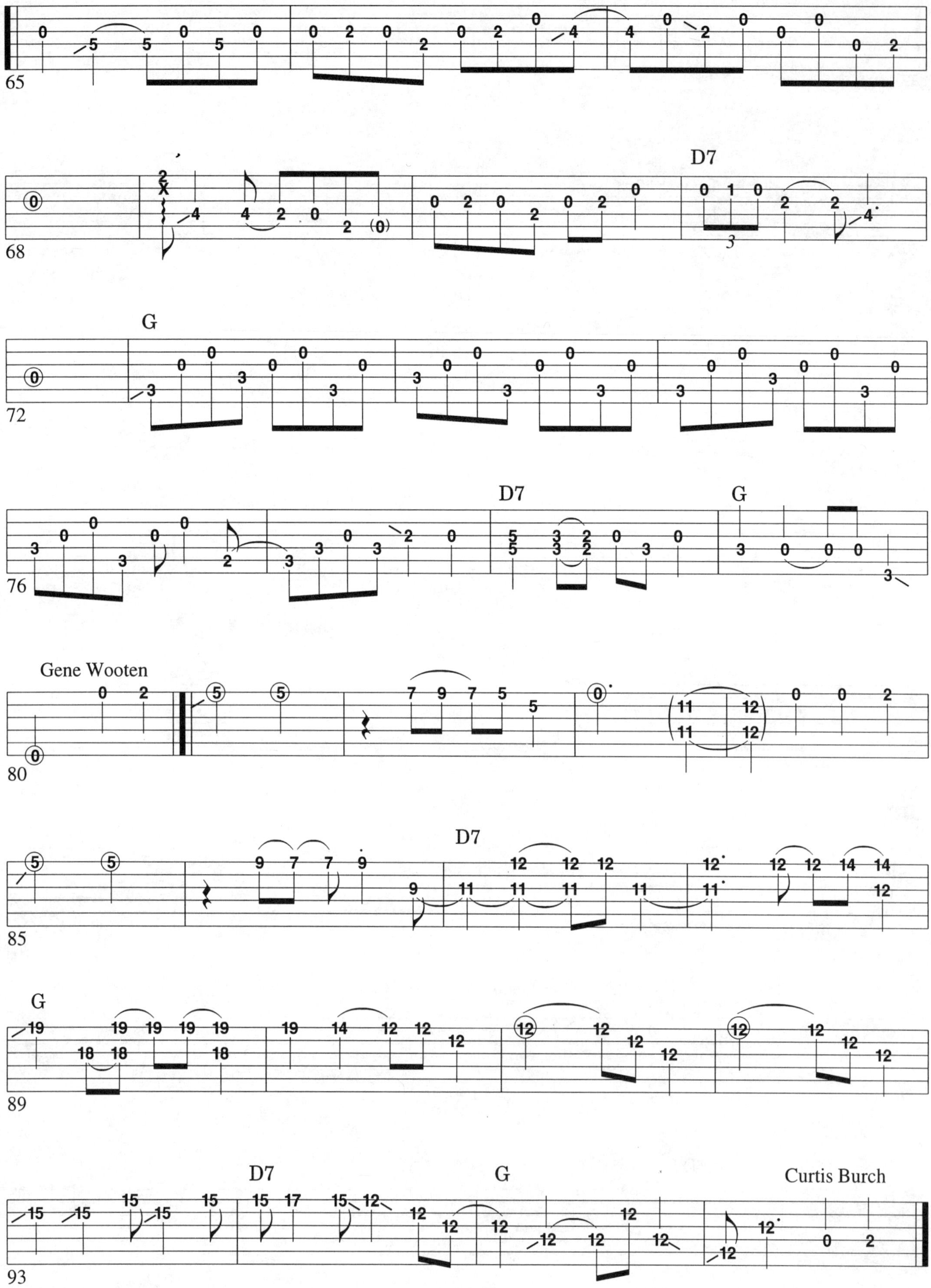
65
68
D7
72
G
76
D7
G
Gene Wooten
80
85
D7
89
G
93
D7
G
Curtis Burch

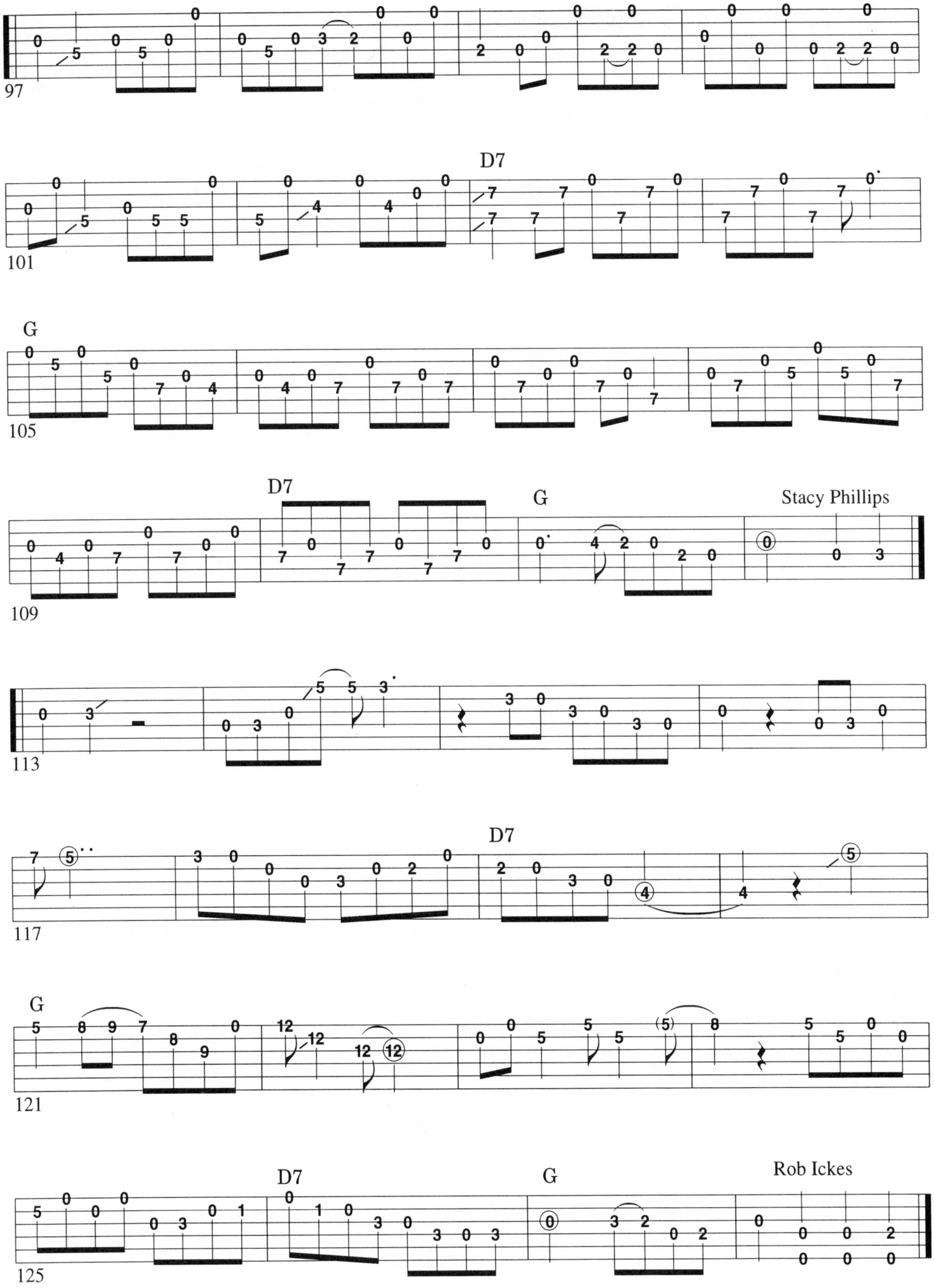
D7
G
D7
G
Stacy Phillips
D7
G
D7
G
Rob Ickes

129
133
D7
G
136
D7
G
Jerry Douglas
140
145
D7
149
G
153
D7
G
156

DOBRO® CHIMES

This is a countrified version of one of the oldest Hawaiian guitar melodies, "Maui Chimes," which in turn was based on a 19th century American children's song called "My Boat Is Sailing." Oswald's third section is not a part of that piece. Roy Acuff's first steel guitarist, Clell "Cousin Jody" Summey recorded it in 1937. Pete Kirby adapted it and made it one of the very few tunes featuring DOBRO® heard in public during the Dark Ages of acoustic steel guitar (ca. 1939-1955).

Kirby is tuned to an open A chord. He plays the same DOBRO® he has used for over fifty years. Using the indicated fretting a guitar tuned to G will be in the key of G, or capo up two frets.

Beware of the 1/4 measure in section 1. This odd timing was already part of the tune on the 1920s recording by Hawaiian ace Sol Hoopii.

Pete "Bashful Brother Oswald" Kirby. (Photo: Jim McGuire.)

DOBRO® CHIMES

As played by Pete Kirby

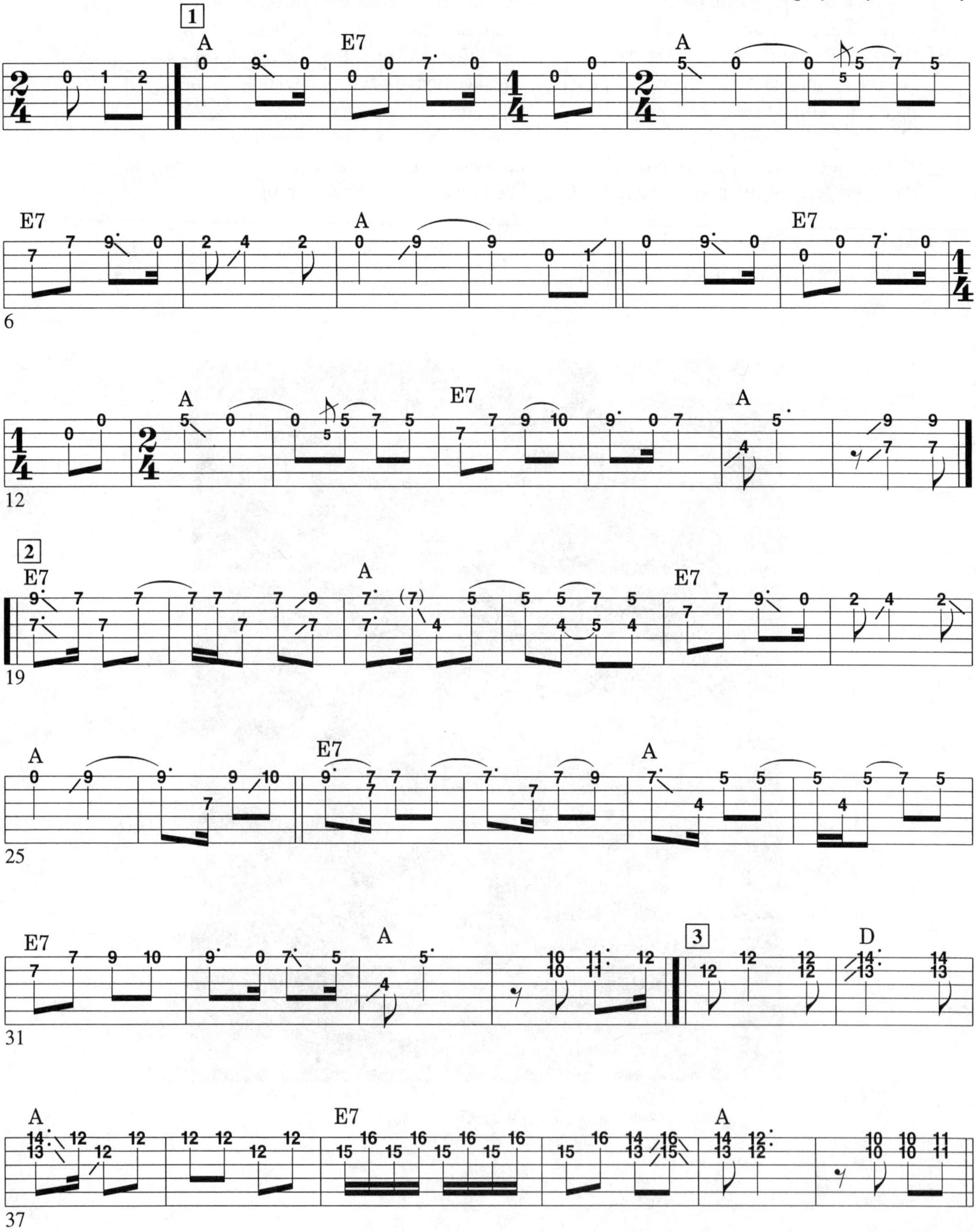

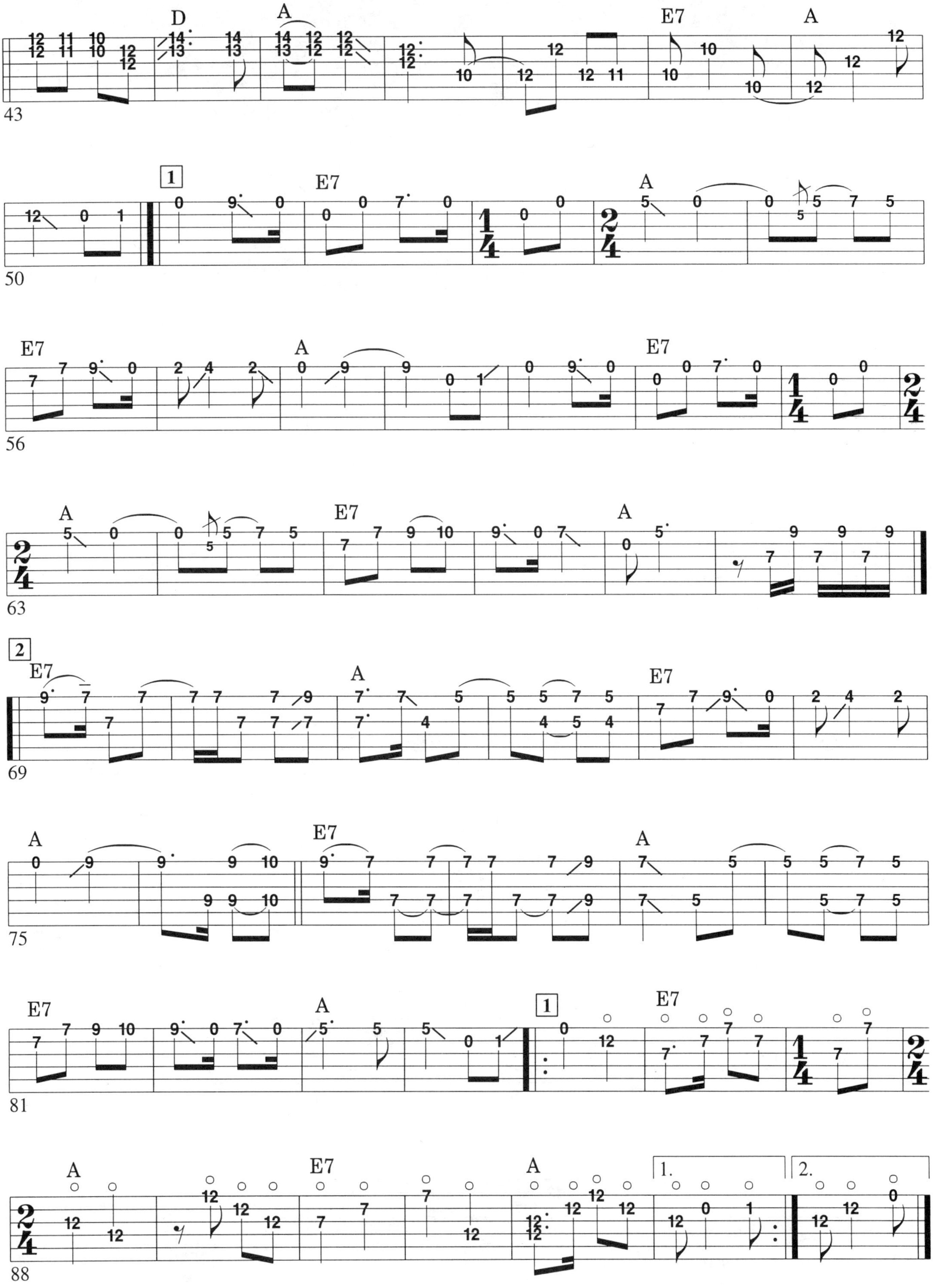

2
E7 A E7
96
A E7 A
102
E7 A 3 D
108
A E7 A
114
D A
120
E7 A 4
125
132
A D A
139
ritard

JUST JOSHIN'

By **Josh Graves**

This was "Josh" Graves' signature tune with Flatt and Scruggs for many years. His association with The Foggy Mountain Boys marked the end of the DOBRO® Dark Ages. It is one of the first pieces that featured Buck's adaptation of Earl Scruggs' banjo style. I still vividly remember the thrill I used to get when he would swoop his guitar upwards toward the microphone, stand on his toes, and whomp into this number.

This is my best guess at all the open string drone-y rolls and arpeggios. At the end of measure 17 Buck plays one of his patented rips, completely deadening the strings around fret 3 or 4, and continuing the strum into the downbeat of the next measure, sliding into the fifth fret.

Buck Graves (photo: Jim McGuire)

JUST JOSHIN'

As played by Buck Graves

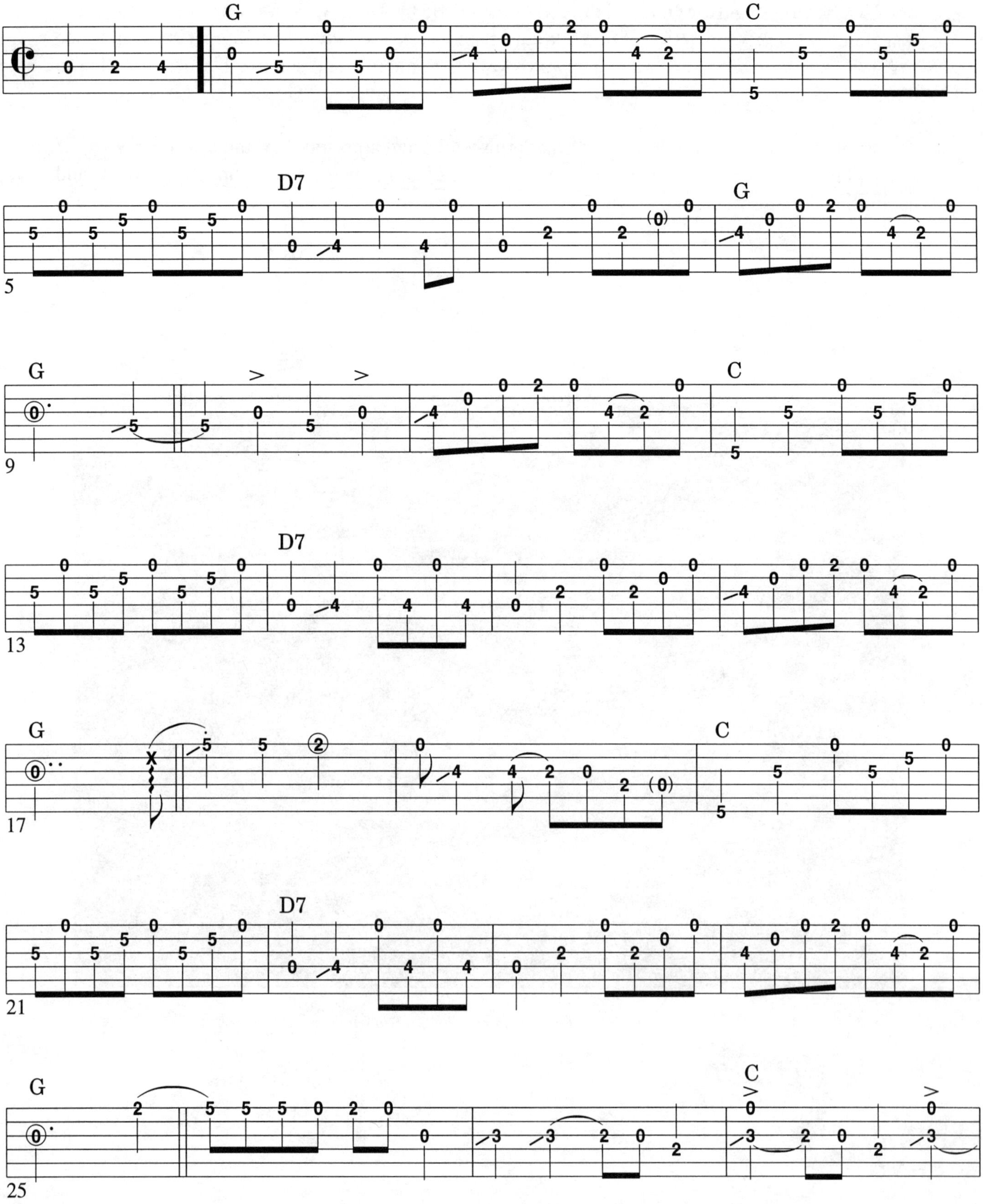

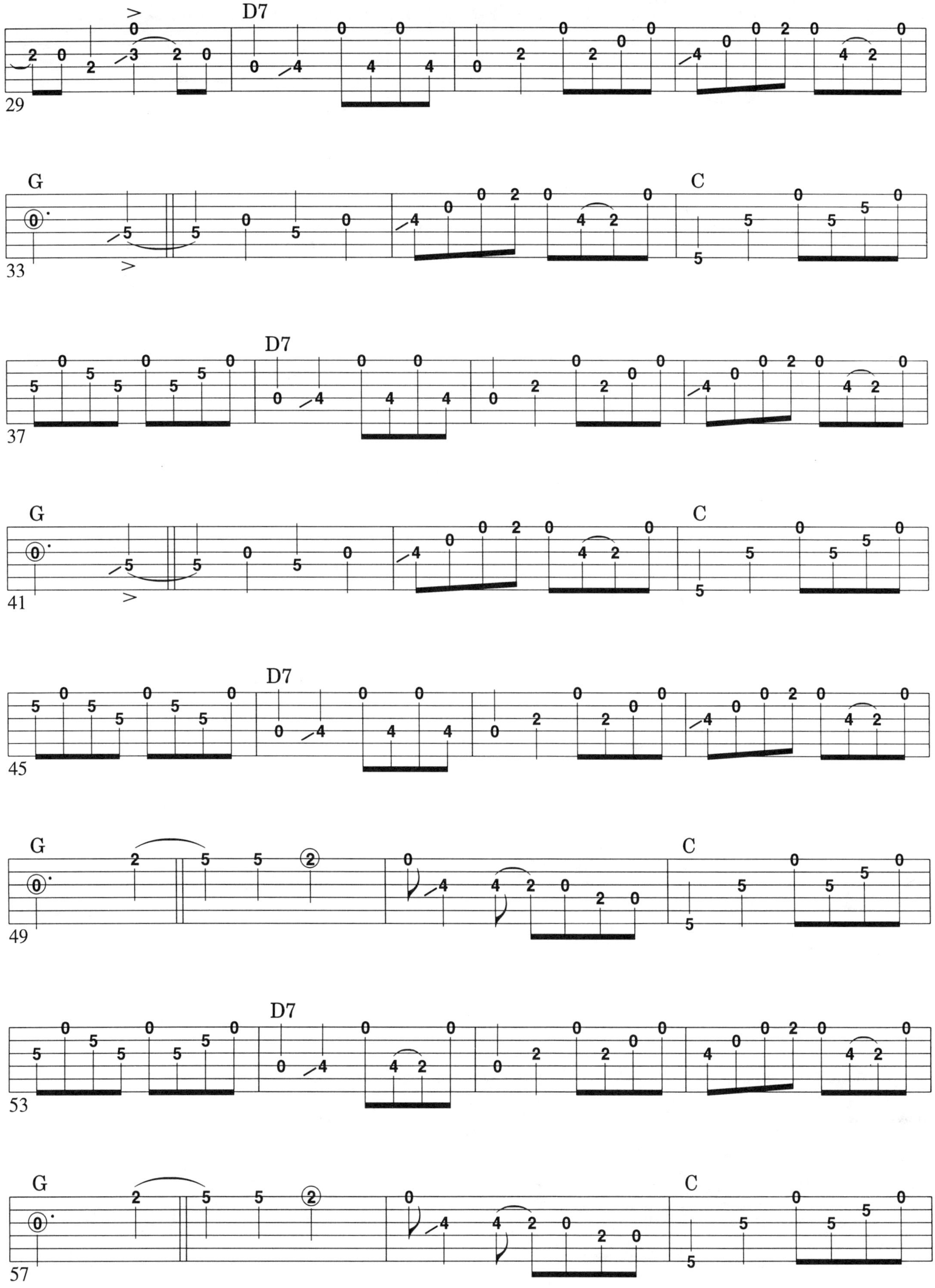
D7
G
C
D7
G
C
D7
G
C
D7
G
C
29
33
37
41
45
49
53
57

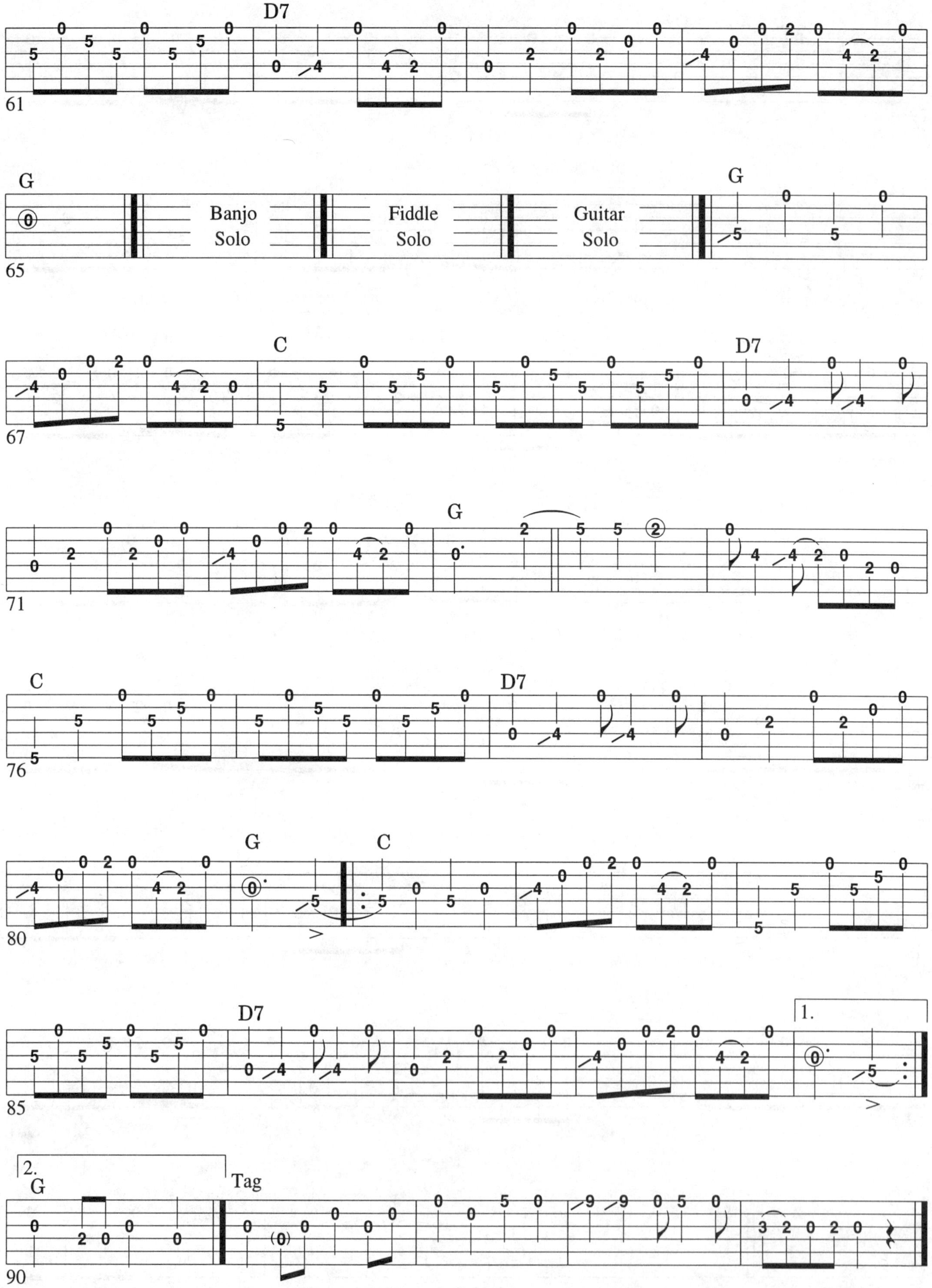
D7
G
Banjo Solo
Fiddle Solo
Guitar Solo
G
C
D7
G
C
D7
G
C
D7
1.
2.
G
Tag

POISON LOVE

Words and Music by **Elmer Laird**

Gene Wooten has combined a bit of Shot Jackson, Buck Graves with his own style in this slant tour de force. The original recording by Johnny and Jack in the early '50s featured Ray "Duck" Atkins on DOBRO®. Jackson soon replaced him in that band.

Follow all the slur and tie lines carefully to get Gene's slippery sound. Often one note of a double stop is picked or slid while the other does something different. Check out measures 10-11 for an extreme example.

In measures 3-4 the double stops might be on the second and fourth string, beginning with S2-F10/ S4-F10. In measure 8 I could only guess at Gene's arpeggiated fill.

The parenthetical S4-F11 indicates the approximate location of the bar on the second beat during the indicated slow slide form F10 to F12.

These guys didn't partake in the album, but this has always been one of my favorite photos. I wish I could hear them play. They were called The Microphonic Four. (Photo: courtesy of Wes Granby)

POISON LOVE

As played by Gene Wooten

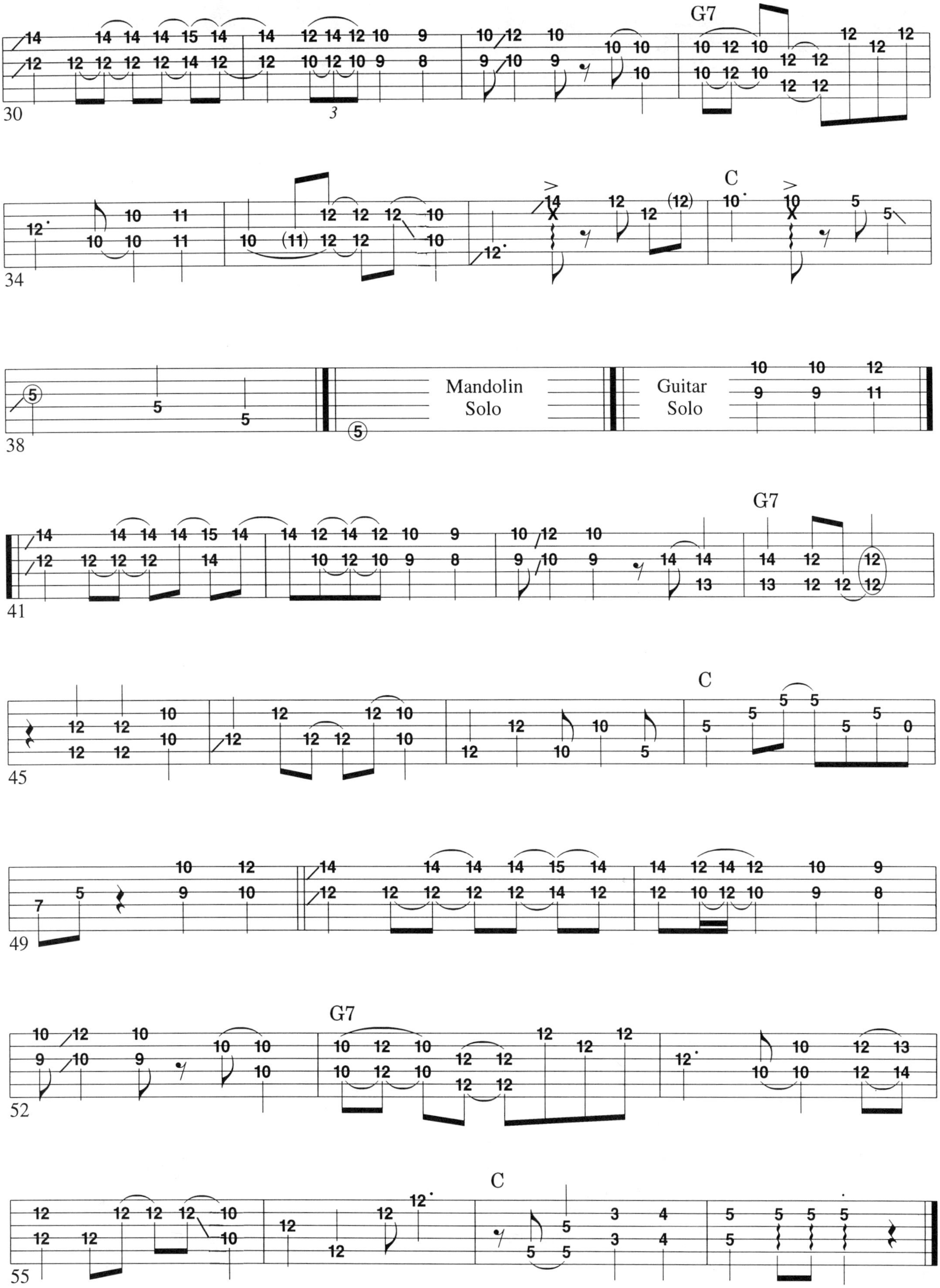
G7
C
Mandolin Solo
Guitar Solo
G7
C
G7
C

BIRDLAND

By **Josef Zawimul**

This is an acoustic string band version of Weather Report's great jazz-fusion arrangement of "Birdland." It is an ensemble piece with little pure soloing. The duplication of parts by more than one instrument is my excuse of choice for inaccuracies in this notation. The chords are a mix of what I heard and the standard progression for the tune as gleaned from *The Real Book.*

There is some noodling in measures 23-24 that I approximated as well as some un-notated arpeggiated fills in measures 38-39 and 42-44 (the latter involves some moves on fret 10 with an open first string) that I also ignored. The stuff on the sixth string in measures 25-26 is partially damped or picked with the very edge of Jerry's thumb pick, i.e. purposeful "mis-hits." Some of the pitches are between frets, so I once again knitted my brow and railed against the inadequacies of music symbols.

Just before section 5 Jerry plays something like what is tabbed in measure 50 for four measures. The seventh section begins similarly. I am unsure if the lick immediately following is played in octaves as notated or with just the highest string. (The bass line makes it difficult to hear.) It does sound cool with the octave.

In section 8 the melody seems to outline the parenthetical chords while the mandolin sticks pretty much with a G7 of some sort.

After section 8 the band returns to section 1, almost duplicating their first pass (beginning with measure 10). The timing is different in the first measure of the return to section 1, then go to the Segno symbol. Jerry leaves out the open first string drone and partially damps his playing with the banjo on repeats 2 and 4. Then section 3 is skipped. Instead section 2 segues into section 4. (The repeated section is then played three times instead of twice.) At that point skip directly to section 6. The last 8 measures of that section (measures 62-69) are played twice leading to the coda.

At this point go directly to the nearest sitz bath for some rehab. I know I needed one after transcribing this load.

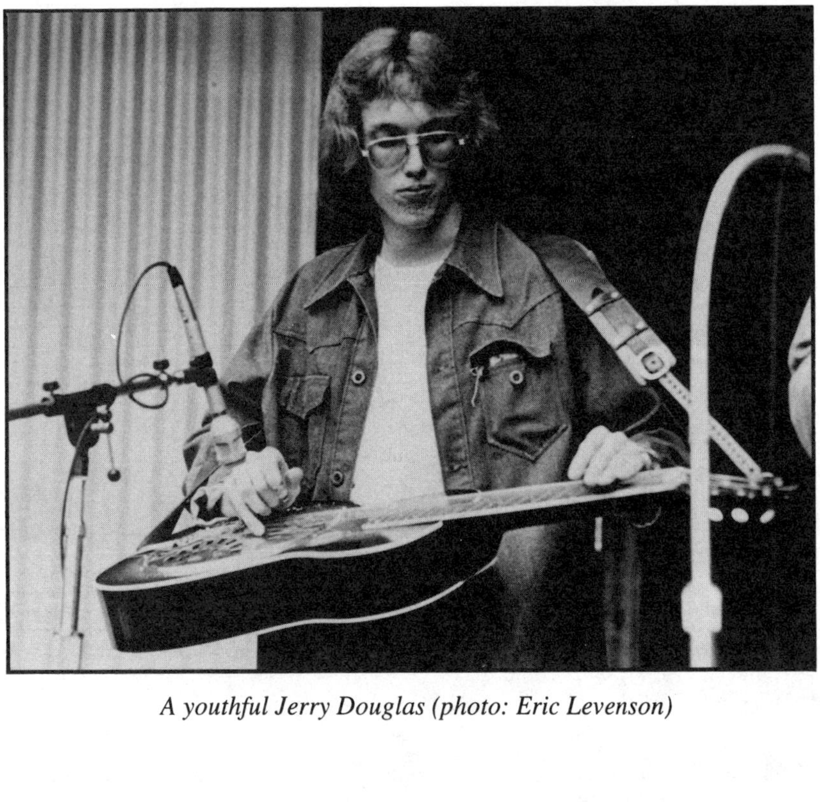

A youthful Jerry Douglas (photo: Eric Levenson)

BIRDLAND

Introduction

As played by Jerry Douglas

4
27
31
1.
2.
35
5
C G
40
C G F
F♯
G7
46
50
6
G Bm Em G C C♯ø Bm E7 Am D7sus
54
G Bm Em C C♯ø Dm C Am G
58

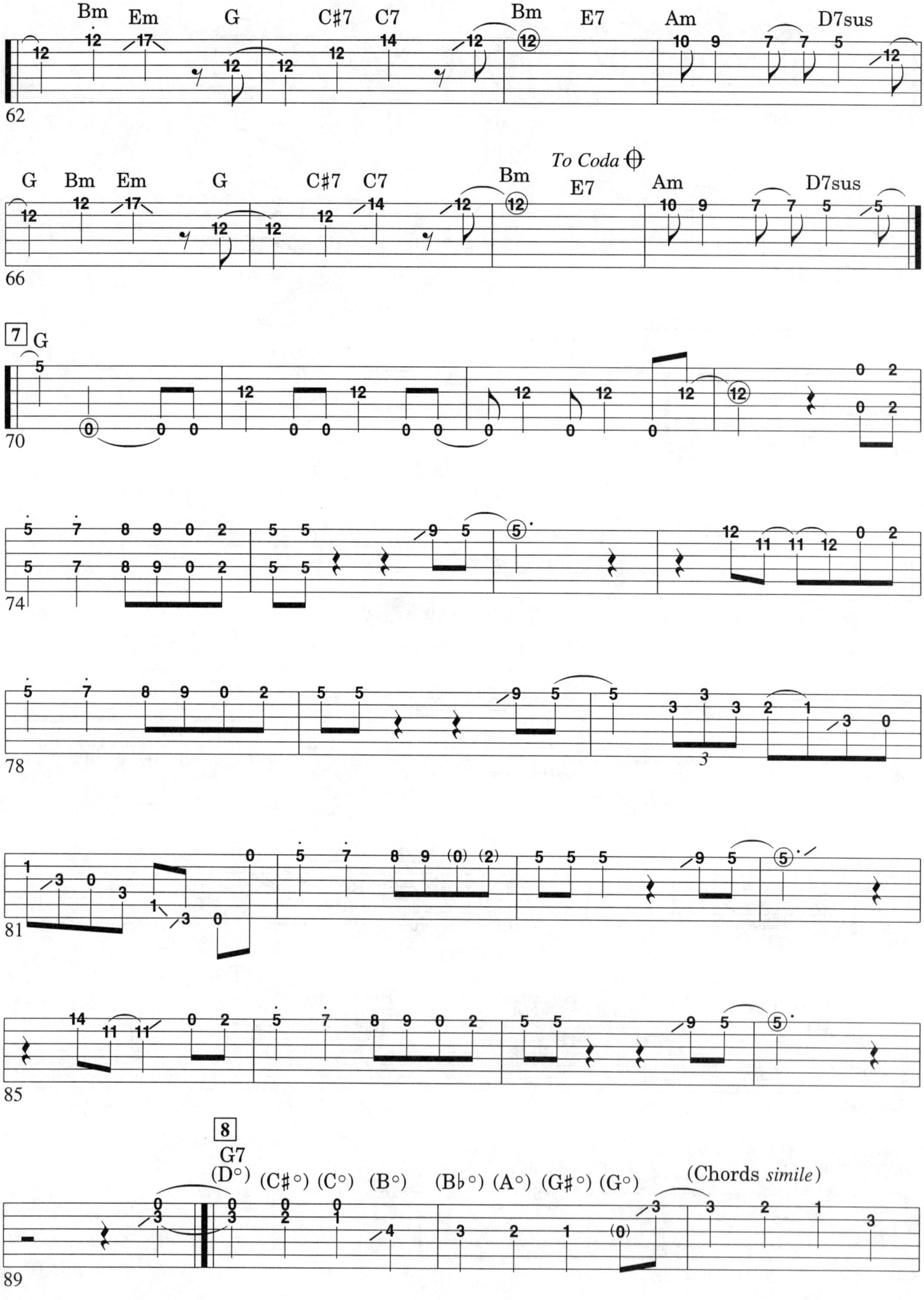
Bm Em G C♯7 C7 Bm E7 Am D7sus
G Bm Em G C♯7 C7 Bm E7 Am D7sus
To Coda
7
G
8
G7
(D°) (C♯°) (C°) (B°) (B♭°) (A°) (G♯°) (G°)
(Chords simile)

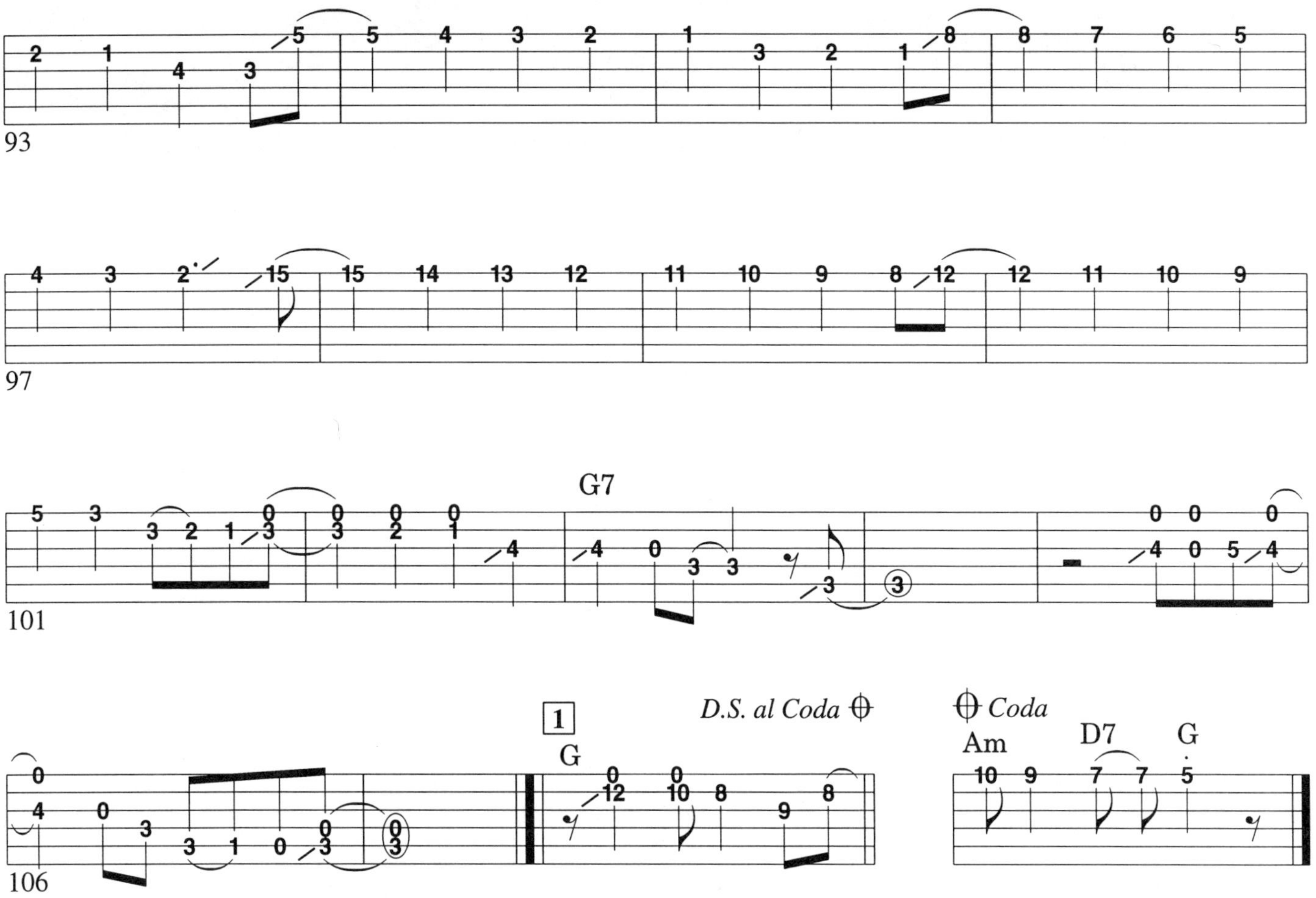
93
97
101
G7
106
1
G
D.S. al Coda
Coda
Am
D7
G

WAVE

By **Antonio Carlos Jobim**

Mike plays this on his R.Q. Jones eight-string resonator guitar tuned to a sort of C6 (from the top D-E [a whole step higher than D]-C-A-G- E-C-A). Since an eight string is a rare bird I have first tabbed it for six string in standard G tuning. The whole steps between Mike's first and second string and also fourth and fifth strings facilitate runs that require much more bar movement in G tuning. In repetitions of some phrases I have tabbed some alternative frettings for your perusal.

After the fiddle solo, the double stop over the F♯7 chord which I have tabbed as S1-F4/S3-F3 actually is translated more precisely to G tuning as S4-F11/S5-F11. However, that would require a big fret jump. My choice allows a smoother flow of notes.

Mike was kind enough to forward an outline of his solo tabbed for the modern C6 tuning he actually used. The first string D was actually the latest wrinkle added to the old Hawaiian-style C6 tuning. It has been adapted to the second neck on currect pedal steel guitars.

There is no rhythm notation so you have to follow along with the recording and use your imagination, because Mike has combined a couple of his variations into one rendition.

Notice that when Mike goes from string two to string one on the 12th fret in this tab, the pitch is going down.

Mike Auldridge with his current band, Chesapeake.

WAVE

As played by
Mike Auldridge

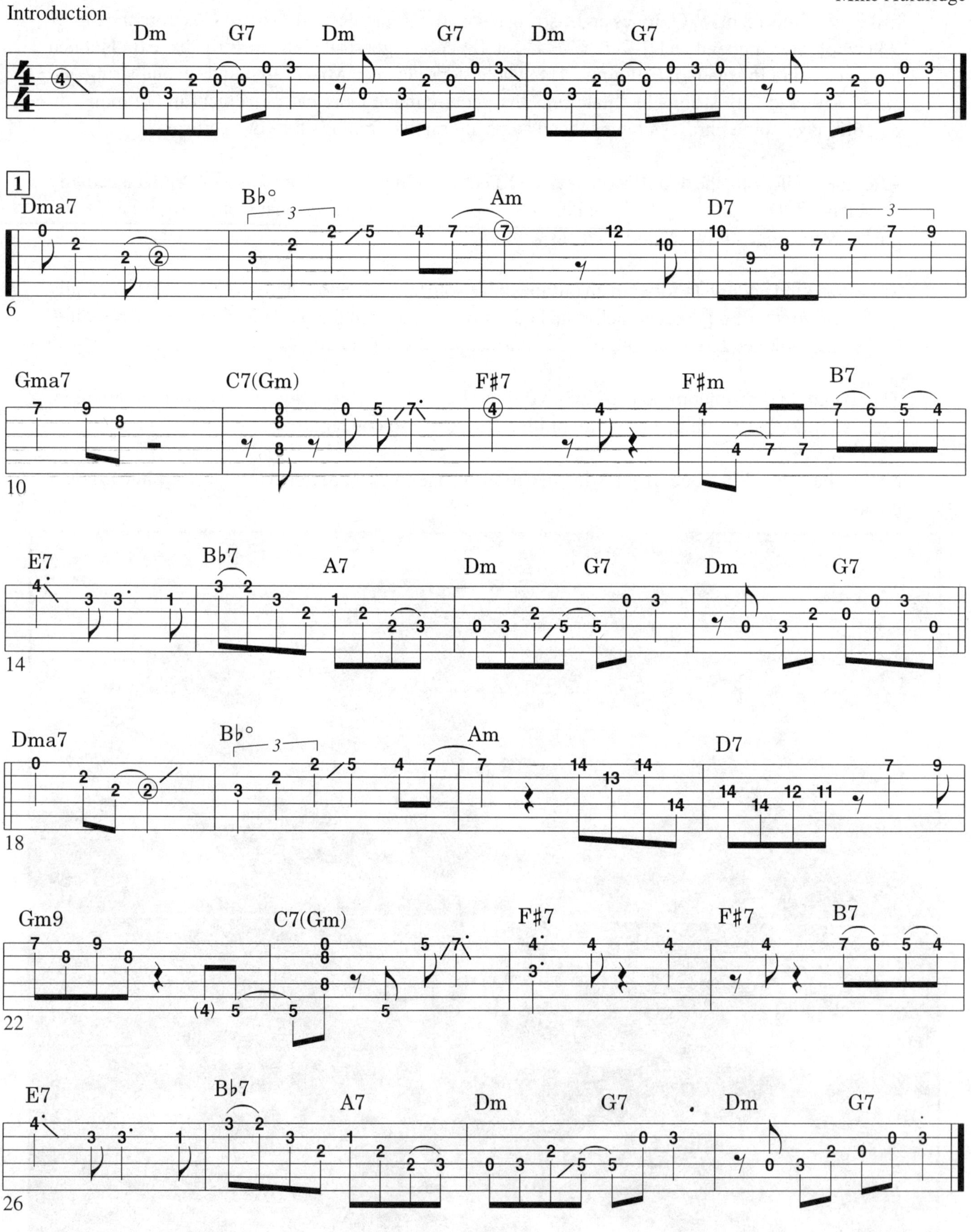

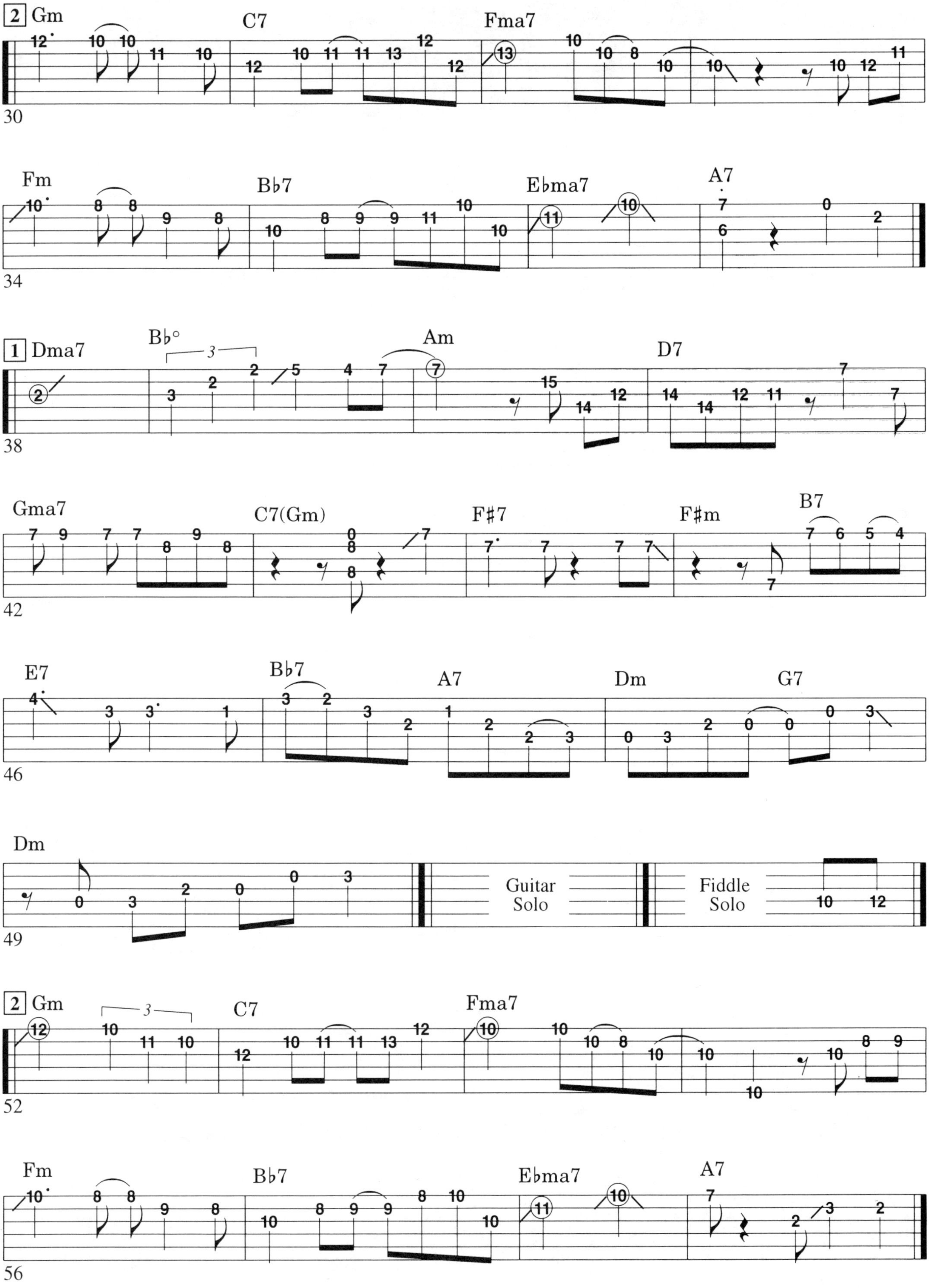
Gm
C7
Fma7
Fm
B♭7
E♭ma7
A7
Dma7
B♭°
Am
D7
Gma7
C7(Gm)
F♯7
F♯m
B7
E7
B♭7
A7
Dm
G7
Dm
Guitar Solo
Fiddle Solo
Gm
C7
Fma7
Fm
B♭7
E♭ma7
A7

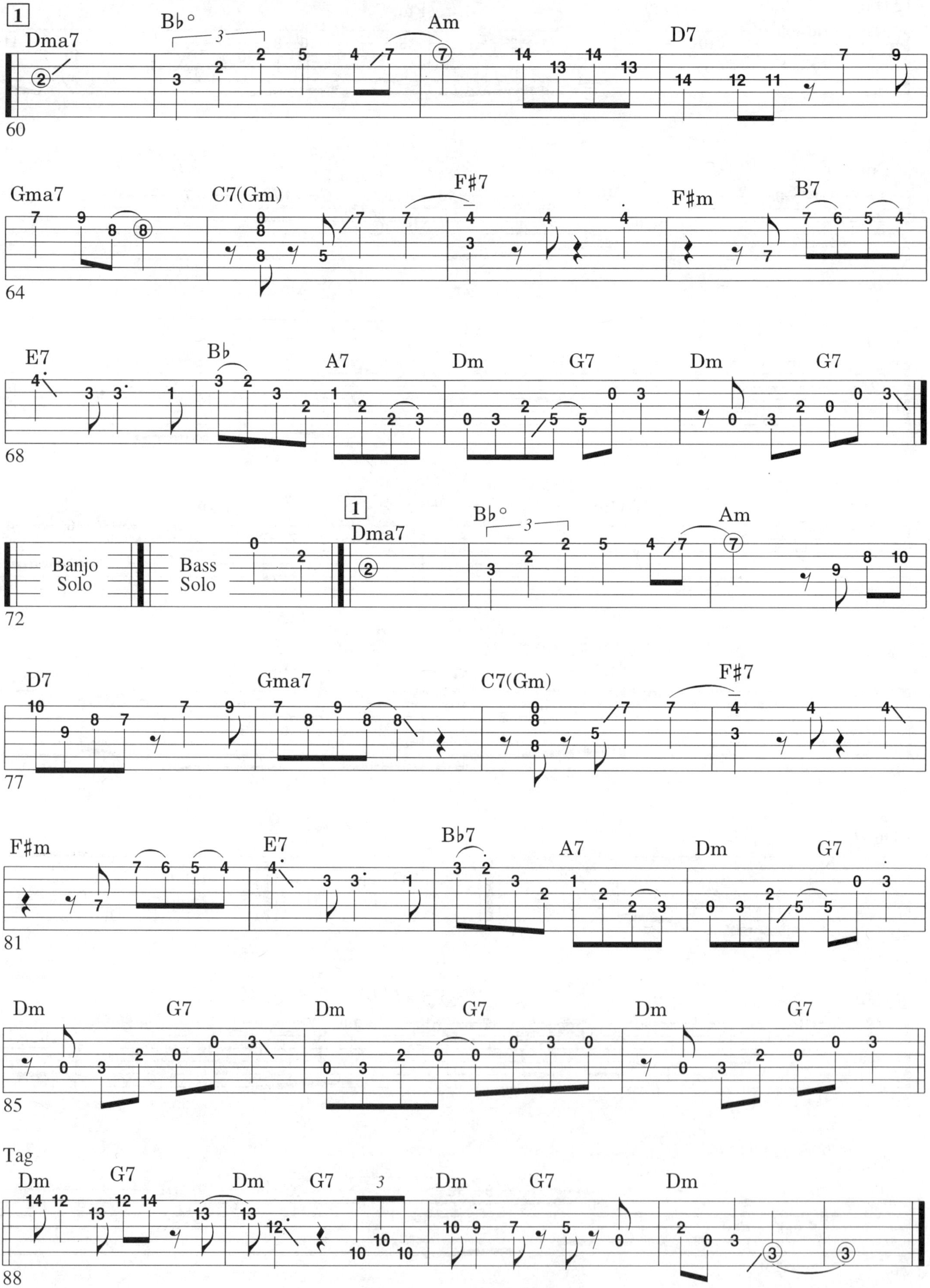
1
Dma7
B♭°
Am
D7
60
Gma7
C7(Gm)
F♯7
F♯m
B7
64
E7
B♭
A7
Dm
G7
Dm
G7
68
Banjo Solo
Bass Solo
1
Dma7
B♭°
Am
72
D7
Gma7
C7(Gm)
F♯7
77
F♯m
E7
B♭7
A7
Dm
G7
81
Dm
G7
Dm
G7
Dm
G7
85
Tag
Dm
G7
Dm
G7
Dm
G7
Dm
88

WAVE

In C6 (+9) tuning

As played by Mike Auldridge

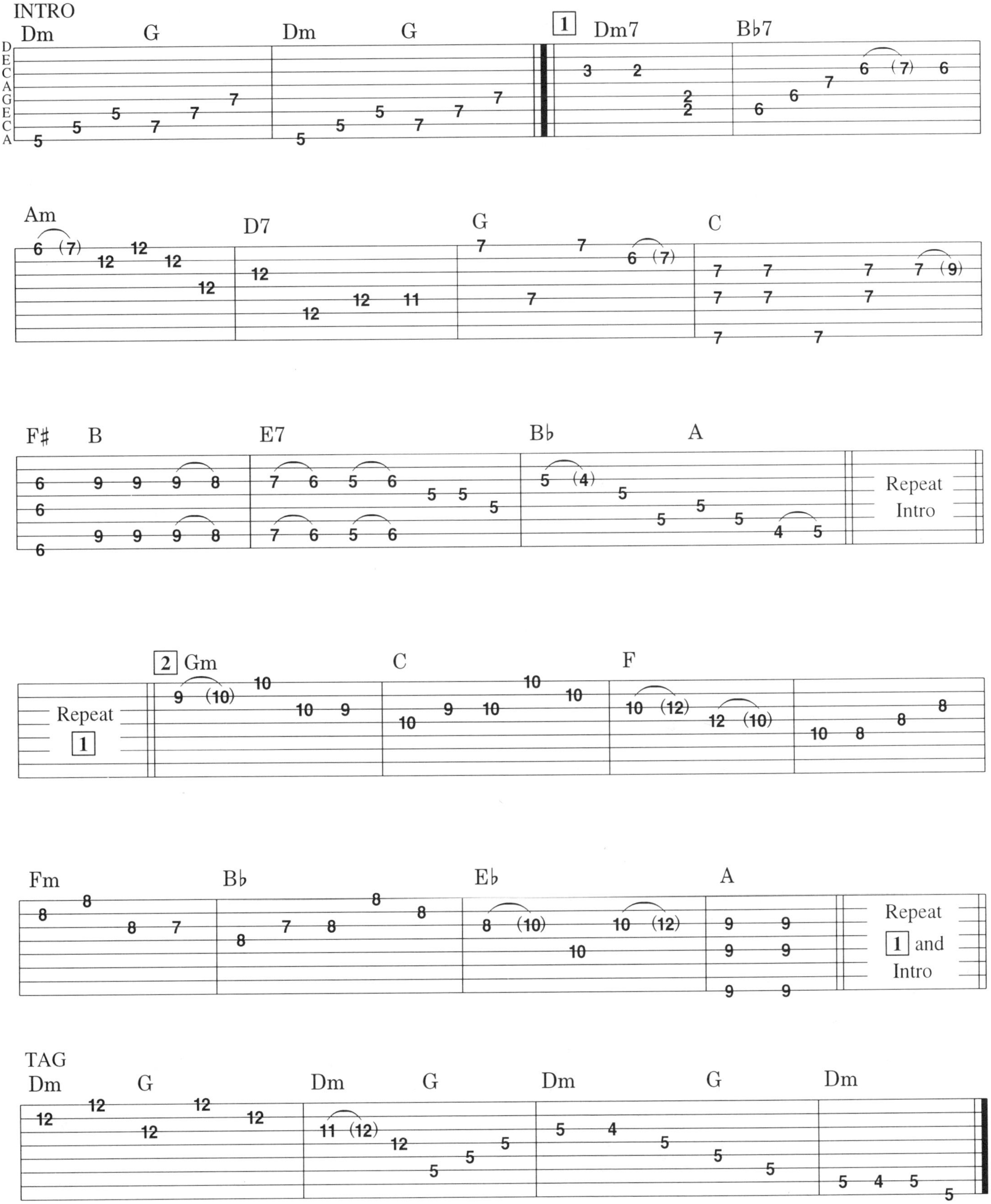

THE LAST ROSE OF AUTUMN

By **Stacy Phillips**

When Jerry Douglas graciously asked me to participate on this project he requested that I do something that featured some chord-melody playing. This tune appeared almost as soon as I got off the phone.

In all of the double and triple stops the melody is the highest pitched note. I go over this tune in detail in my Homespun video tape *DOBRO® Repertoire and Technique #2.*

After recording the Hey Mister Get the Ball *album. From left: Marty Confurius, Jon Sholle, Stacy Phillips, Andy Statman; seated: Bishop O'Brien. (Photo: Gale Justin)*

THE LAST ROSE OF AUTUMN

As played by Stacy Phillips

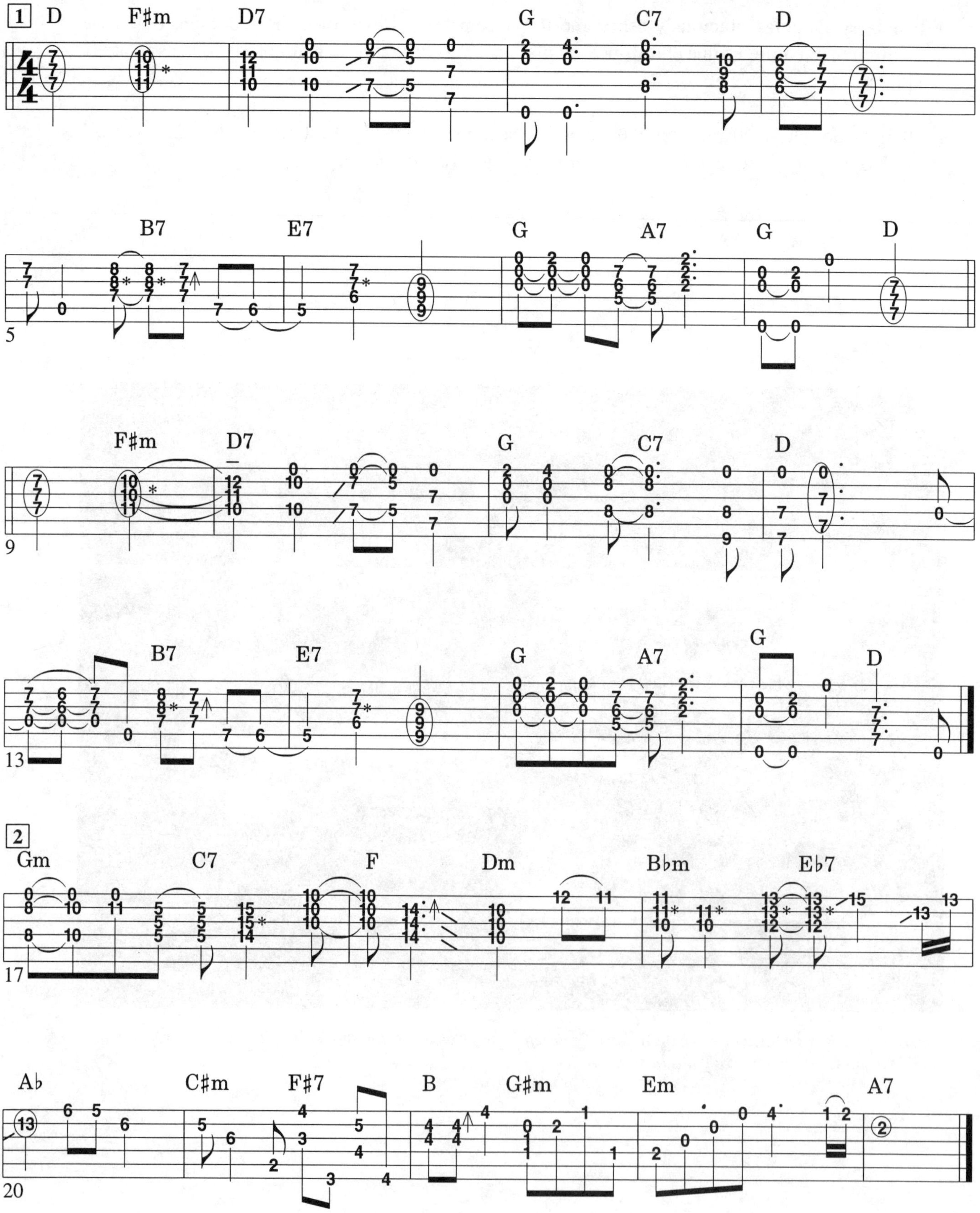

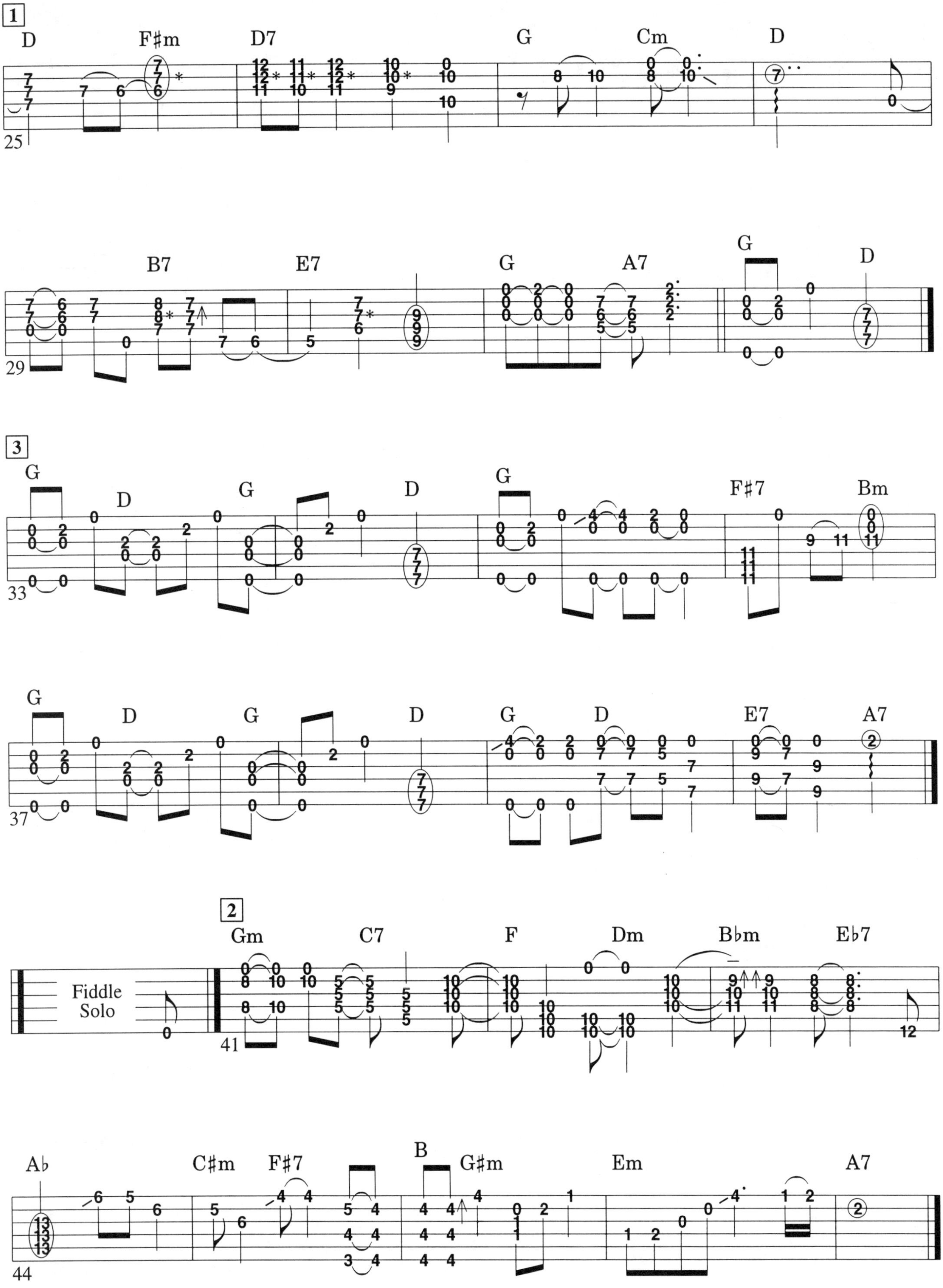
1
D F♯m D7 G Cm D
B7 E7 G A7 G D
3
G D G D G F♯7 Bm
G D G D G D E7 A7
Fiddle Solo
2
Gm C7 F Dm B♭m E♭7
A♭ C♯m F♯7 B G♯m Em A7

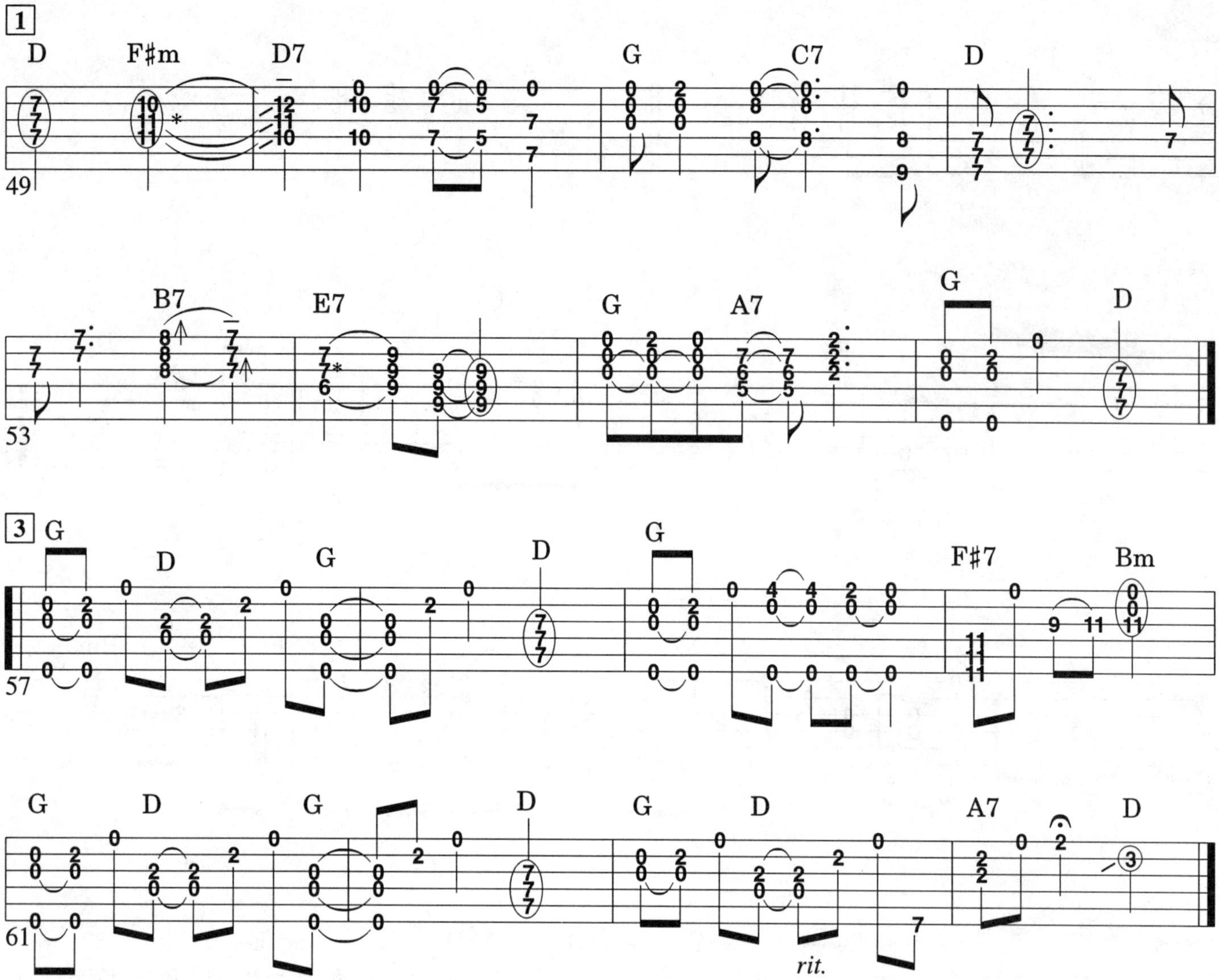
1
D F#m D7 G C7 D
B7 E7 G A7 G D
3
G D G D G F#7 Bm
G D G D G D A7 D
rit.

RAINBOW BRIDGE

By **Curtis Burch**

Curtis occasionally played lap slide with the original New Grass Revival. (His main instrument is still flat top guitar.) One of their most memorable arrangements featured his slide with Sam Bush's bottleneck mandolin on Tut Taylor's original "Little Green Pill." Whenever Sam would ask, "What time is it?," the audience would respond, "DOBRO® time!" and Curtis would launch into "Rainbow Bridge."

Curtis Burch (photo courtesy Burch Family collection)

RAINBOW BRIDGE

As played by
Curtis Burch

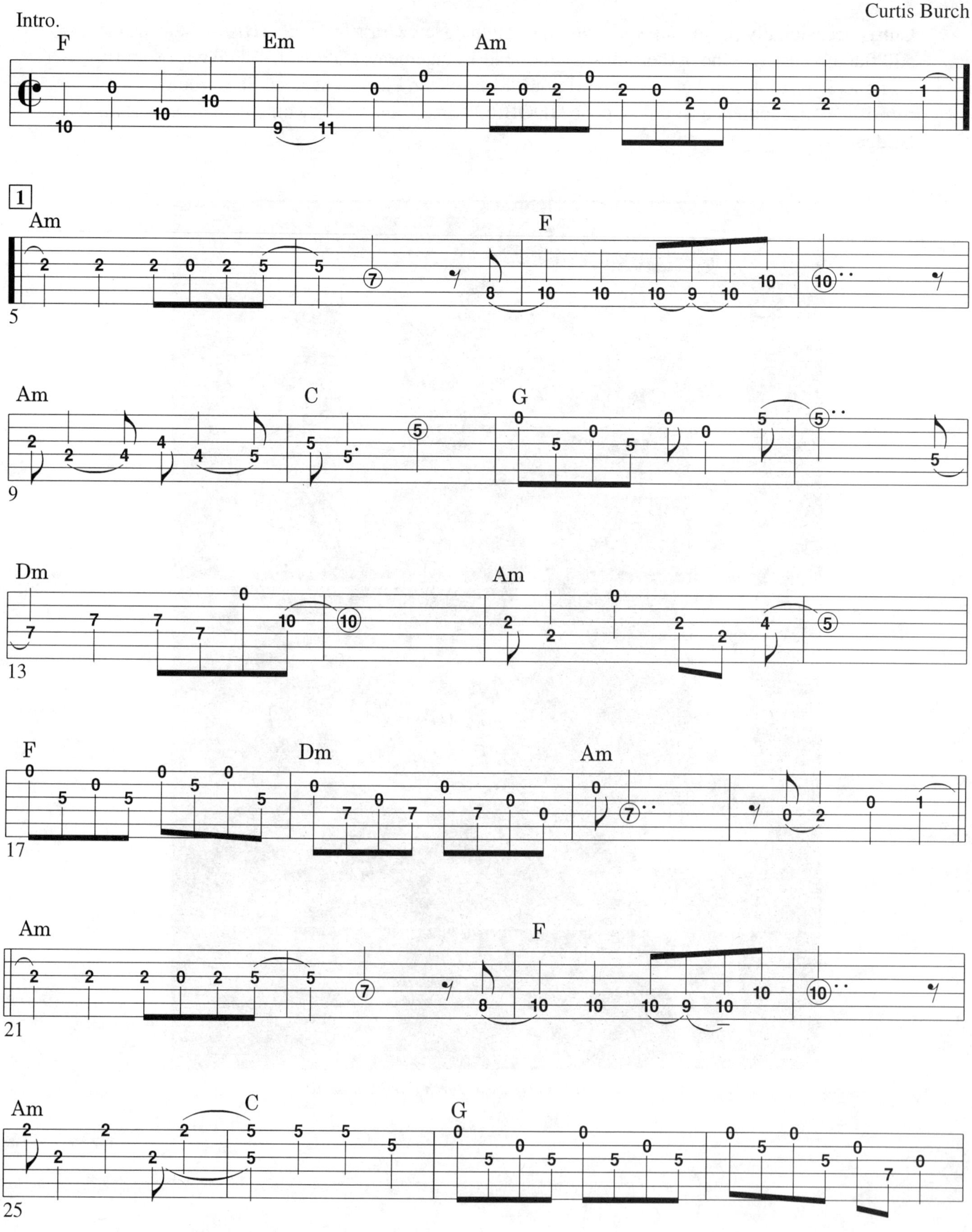

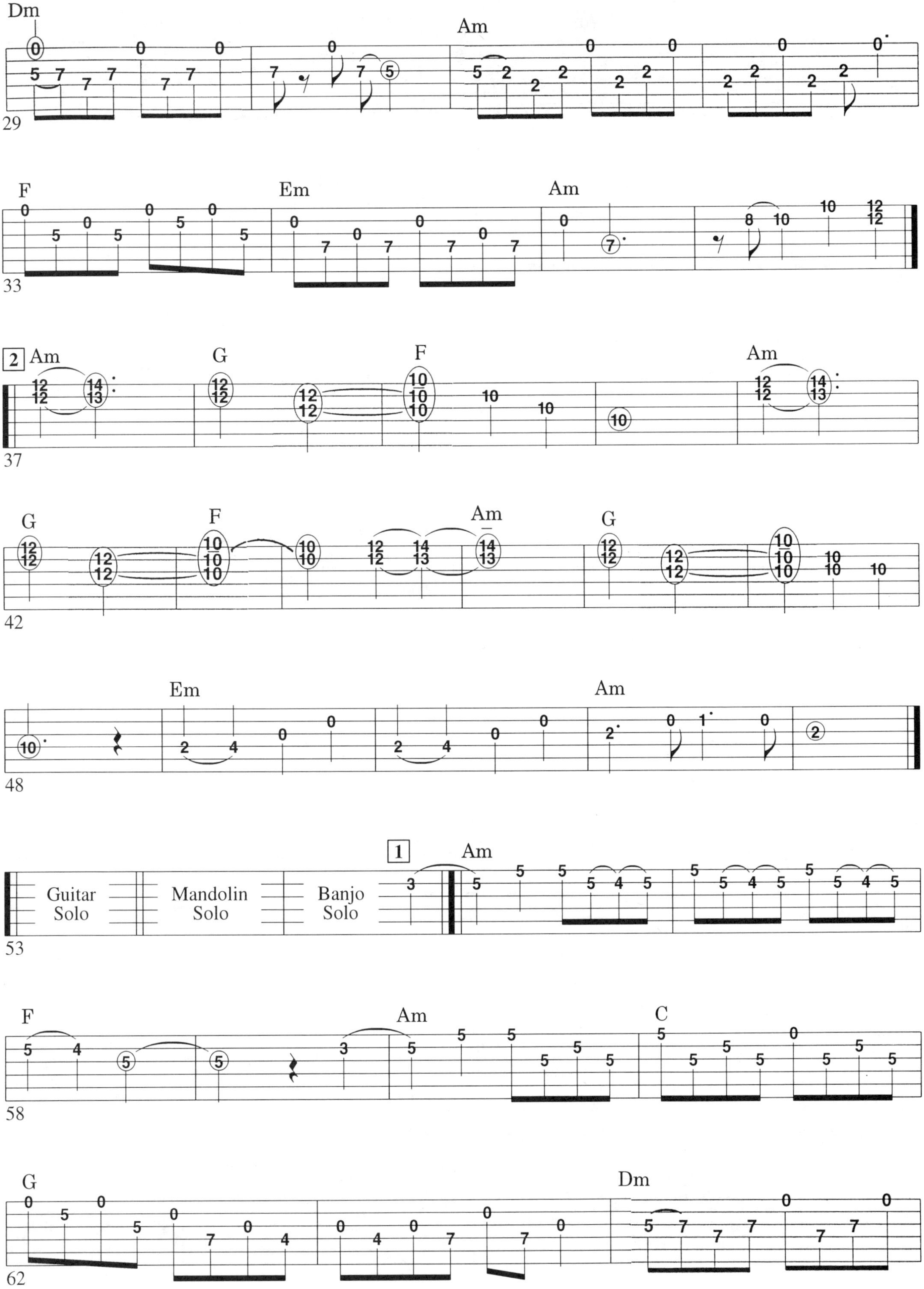

Dm
Am
F
Em
Am
2
Am
G
F
Am
G
F
Am
G
Em
Am
Guitar Solo
Mandolin Solo
Banjo Solo
1
Am
F
Am
C
G
Dm

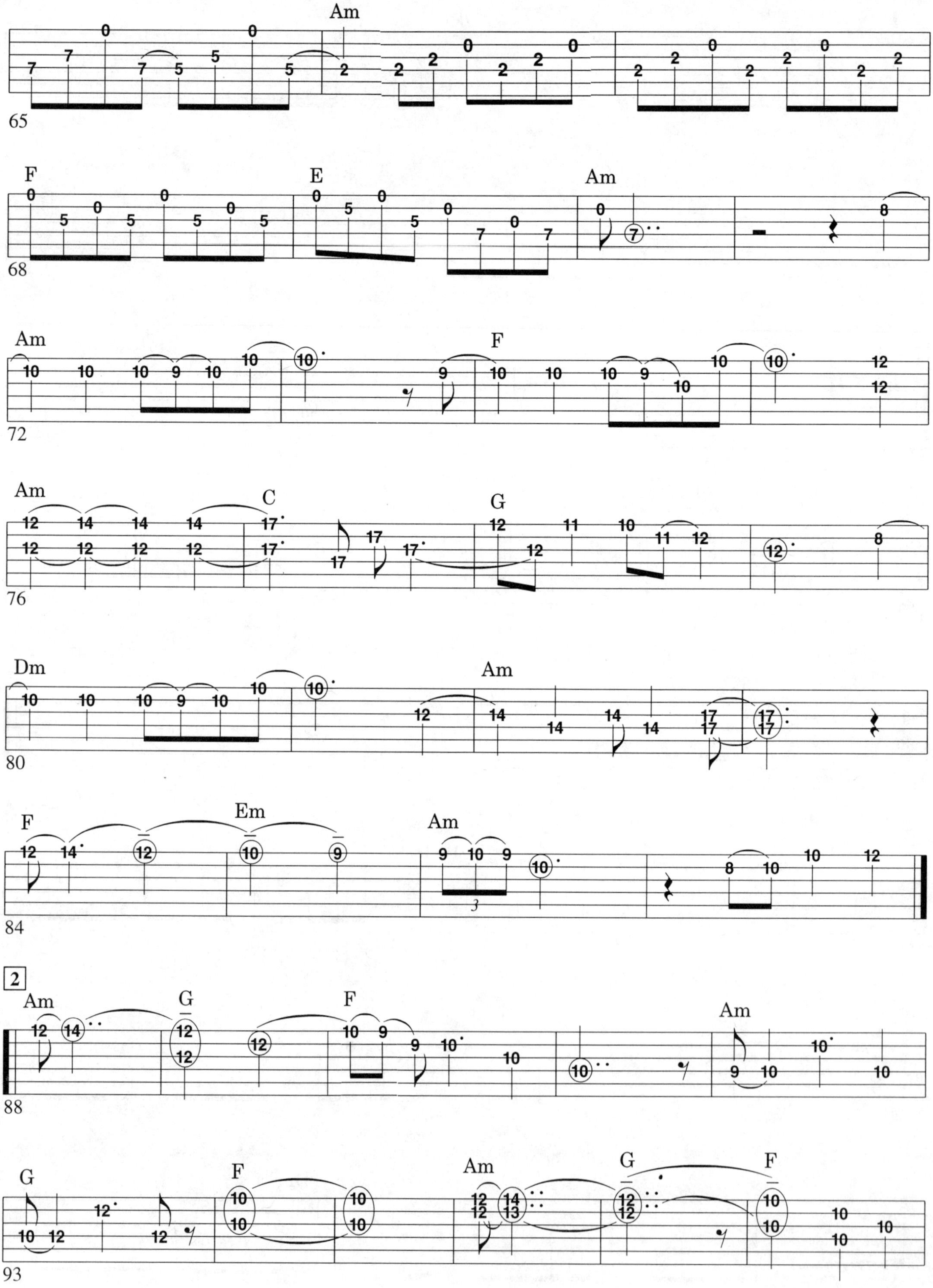
Am
65
F
E
Am
68
Am
F
72
Am
C
G
76
Dm
Am
80
F
Em
Am
84
2
Am
G
F
Am
88
G
F
Am
G
F
93

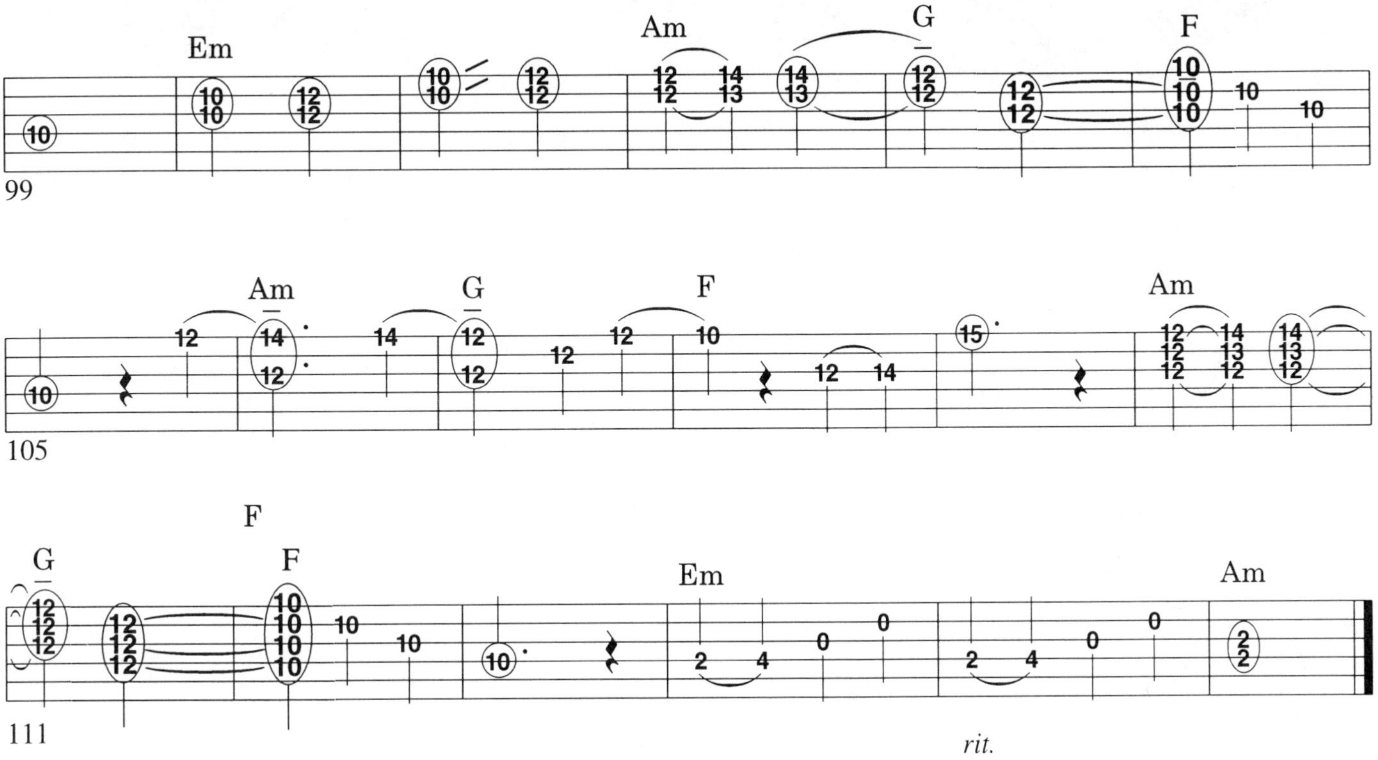

Em
Am
G
F
99
Am
G
F
Am
105
G
F
F
Em
Am
111
rit.

GREAT SEASON WALTZ

By **Slavek Hanzlik**

This tune was written by Slavik Hanzlik from the Czech Republic, which is right next to the Slovak Republic, the birth place of the Dopjera brothers for whom the DOBRO® is named. Sally uses it to confirm her mastery of touch and tone on her Scheerhorn resonator guitar.

There are plenty of alternatives to the barring patterns I have chosen. I have even notated different ones for the same lick as in measures 5 and 13. The last riff, beginning with the fermata on the F♯ chord, is another one whose exact fretting escaped me. As usual some arpeggiated fills were unclear to me.

Sally Van Meter (photo by Irene Young)

GREAT SEASON WALTZ

As played by Sally Van Meter

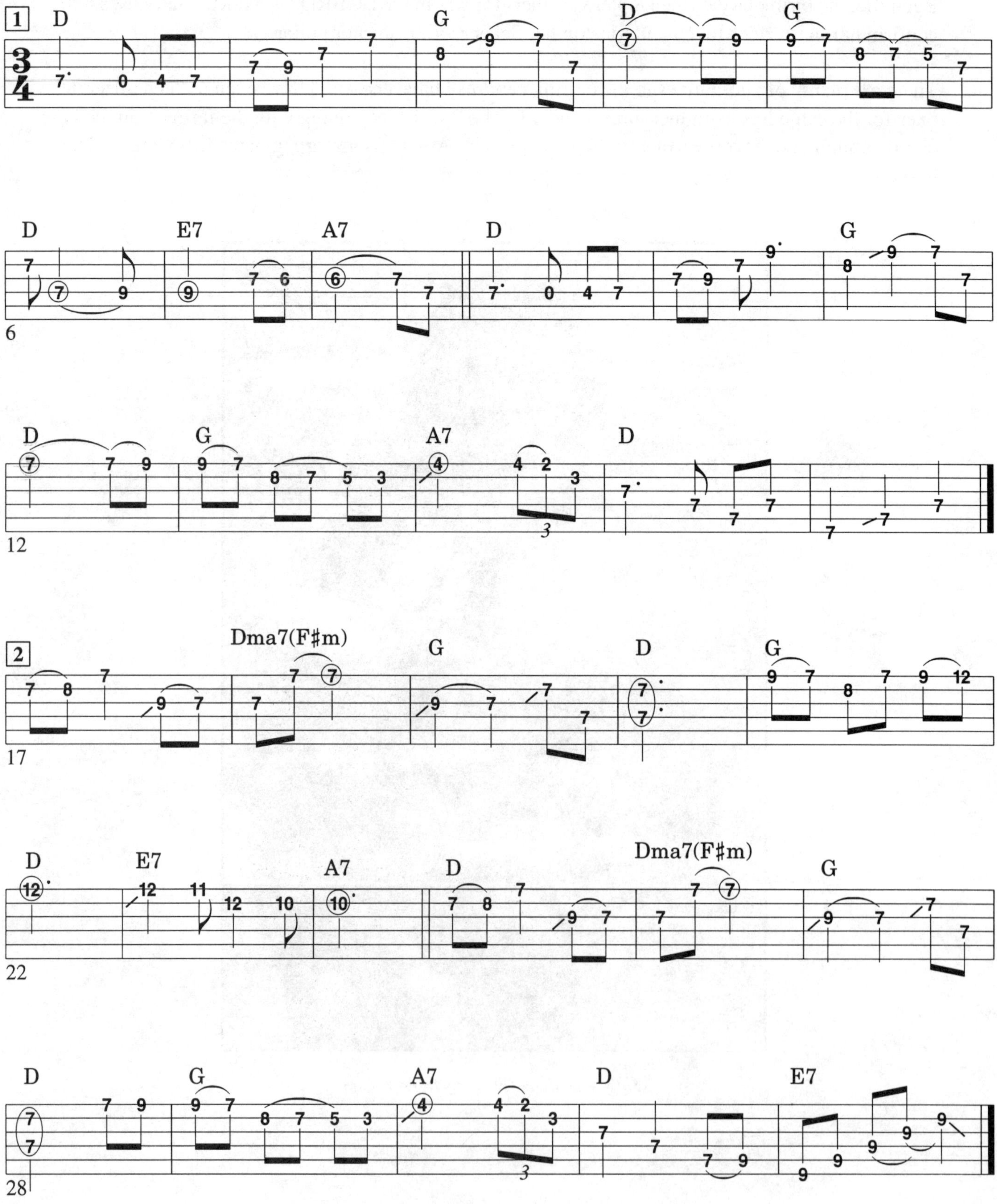

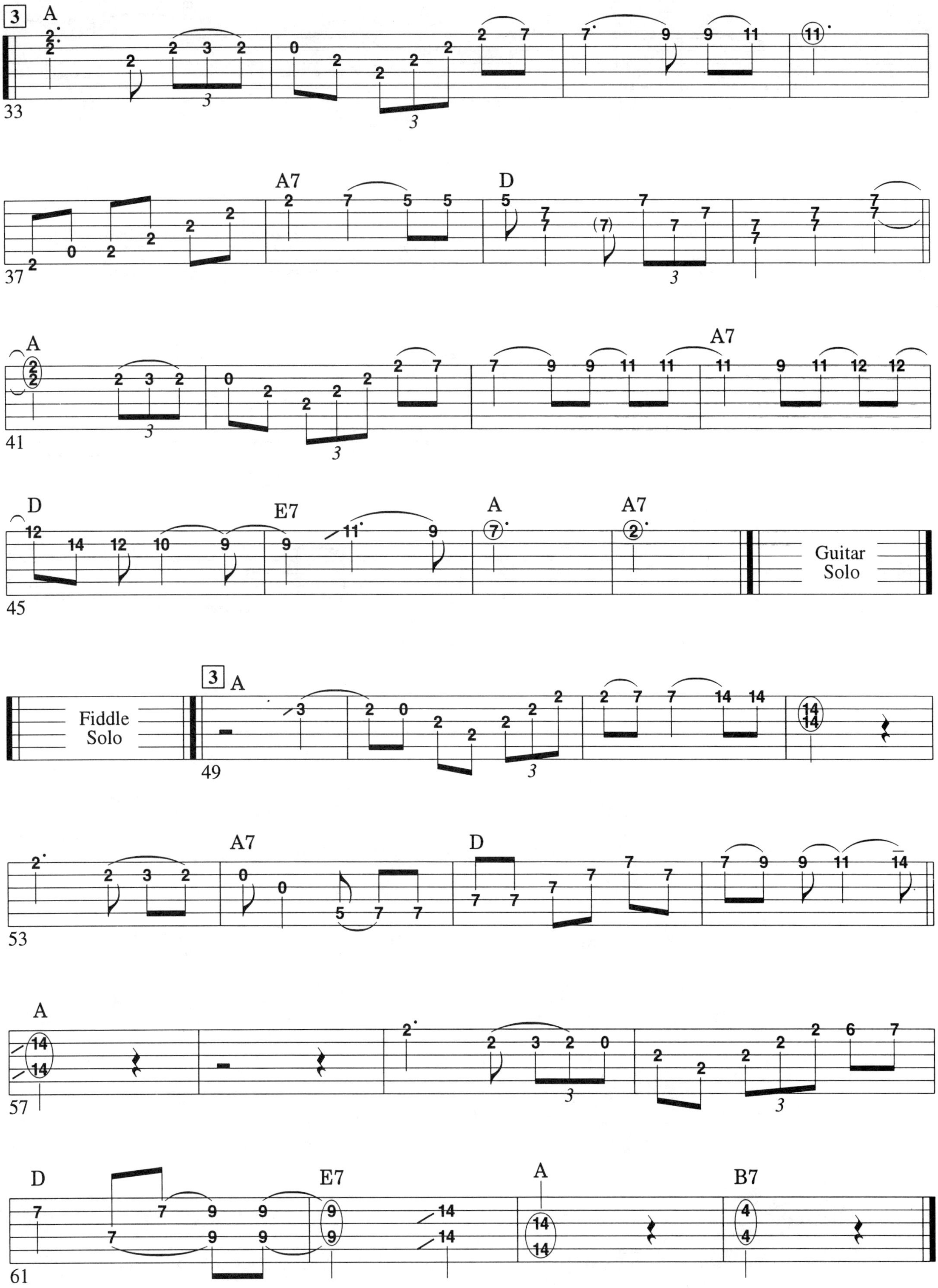
A
A7
D
A
A7
D
E7
A
A7
Guitar Solo
Fiddle Solo
A
A7
D
A
D
E7
A
B7

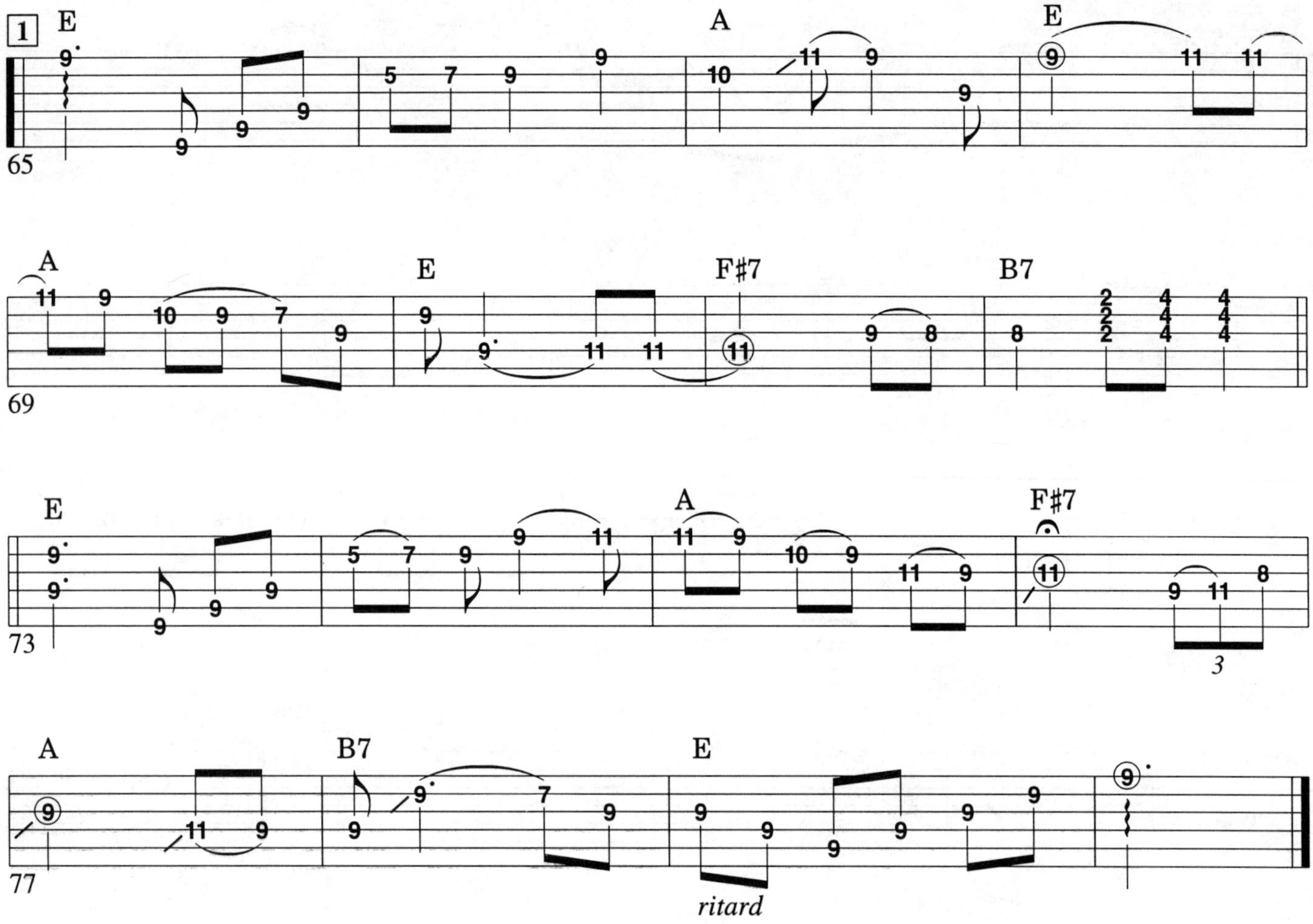
1
E
A
E
65
A
E
F#7
B7
69
E
A
F#7
73
A
B7
E
77
ritard

SCRAPIN' THE BARREL

By **Rob Ickes**

Many of Rob's open string rolls are hard to decipher. Try your luck with his introduction and the last measure of section 1, just before the first version of section 3. His rolls are so rapid fire that some of this transcription is based purely on my imagination. A couple of the long notes in section 2 are probably parts of rolls that are too far down in the audio mix to decipher.

In the final measure it sounds like Ickes makes a completely damped strum as a pitchless exclamation point, followed by a final slide.

Rob assures me that I gave him a lesson in his pre-puberty days. If that is so he has made a remarkable recovery to become an outstanding, driving steel guitarist.

Rob Ickes.

SCRAPIN' THE BARREL

As played by Rob Ickes

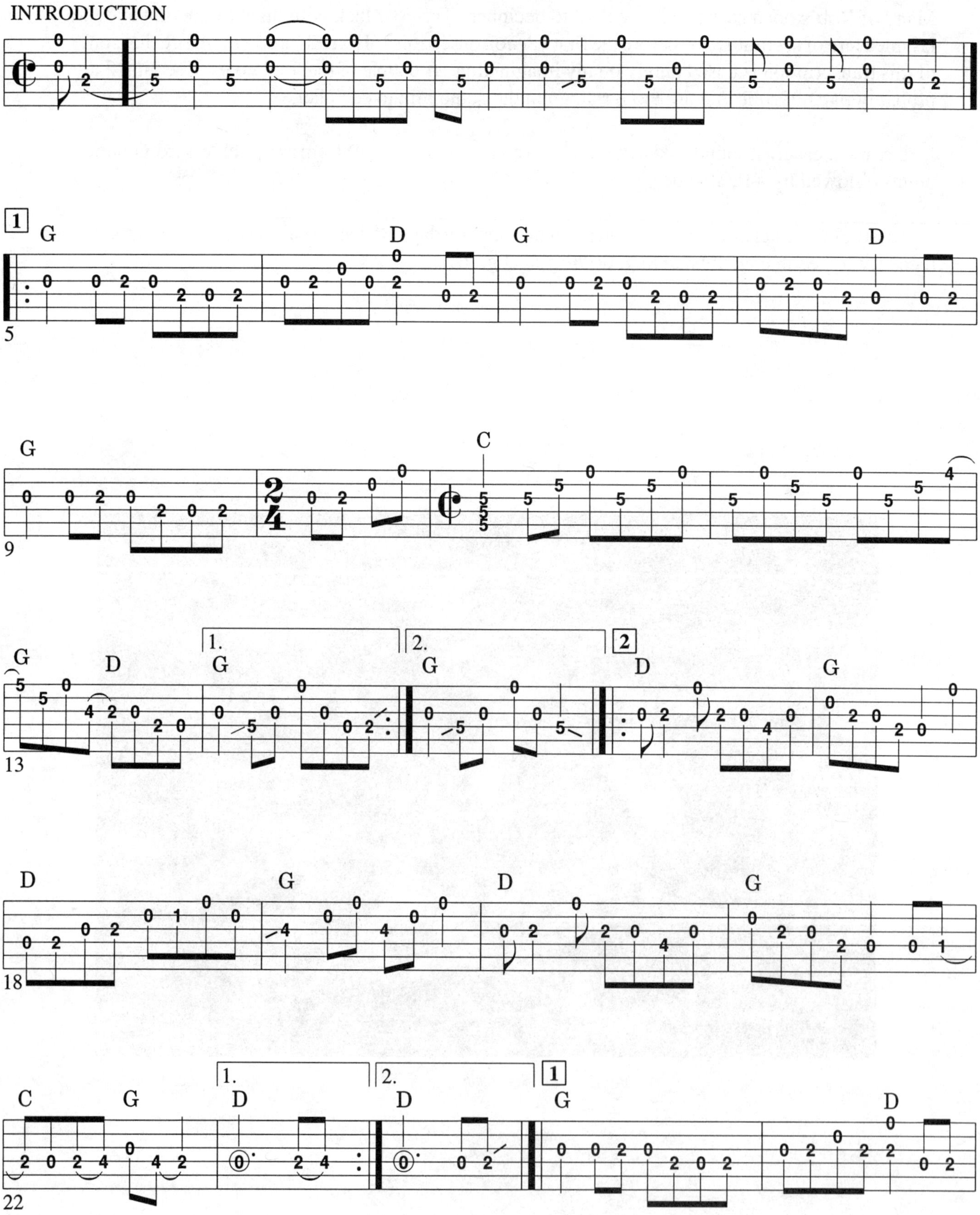

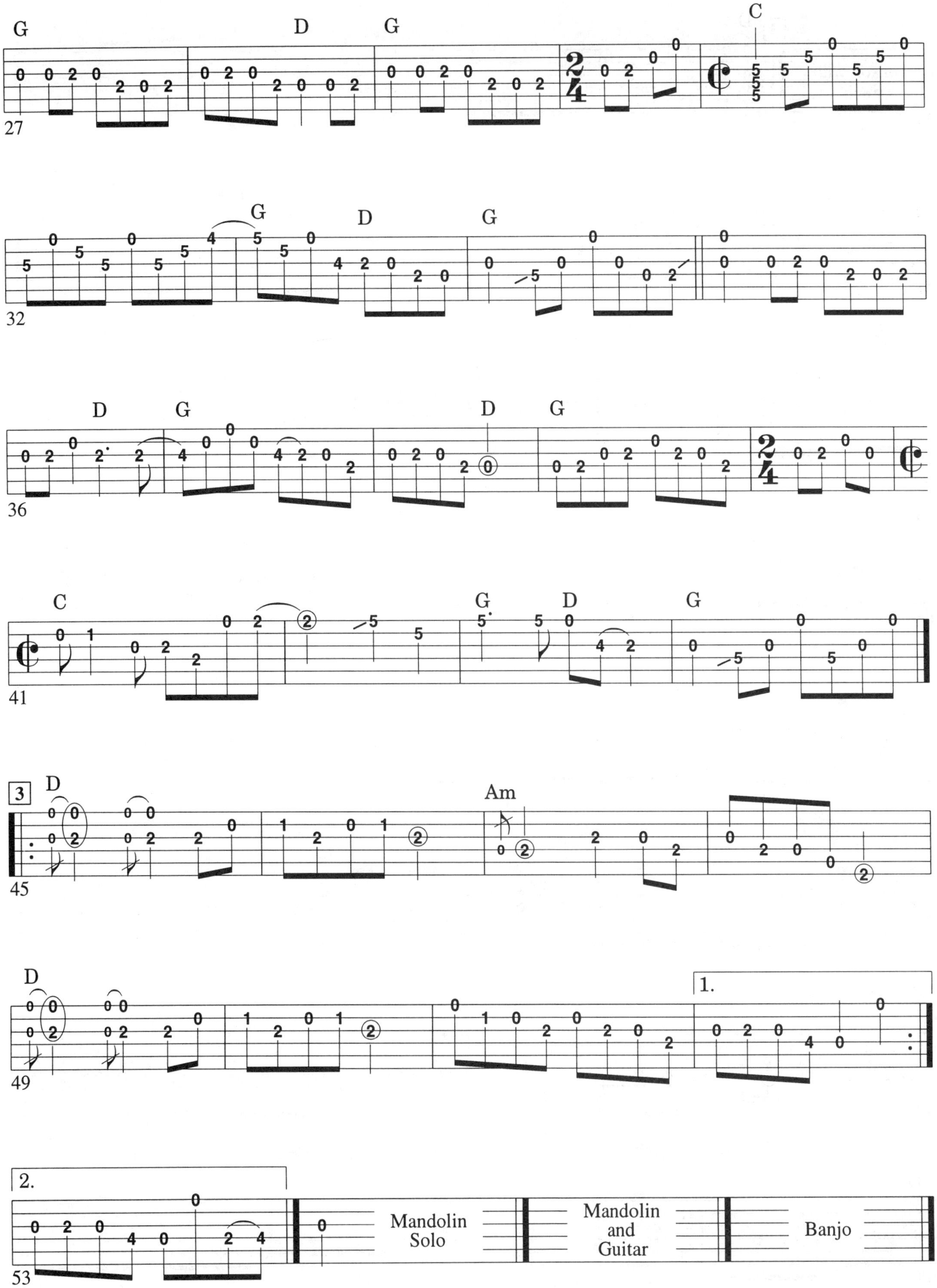
G D G C
27
G D G
32
D G D G
36
C G D G
41
3
D Am
45
D
1.
49
2.
53
Mandolin Solo
Mandolin and Guitar
Banjo

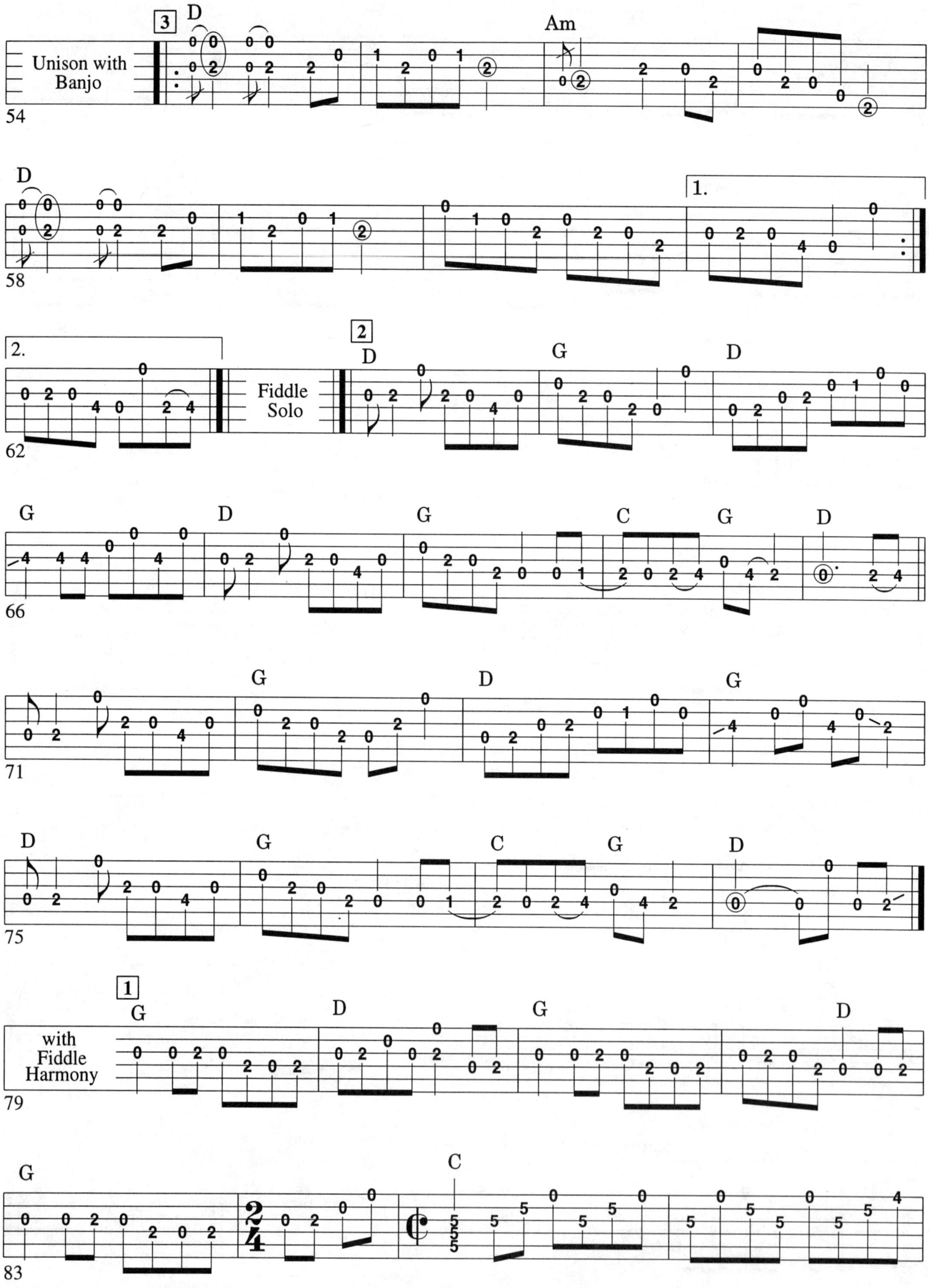
Unison with Banjo
Fiddle Solo
with Fiddle Harmony

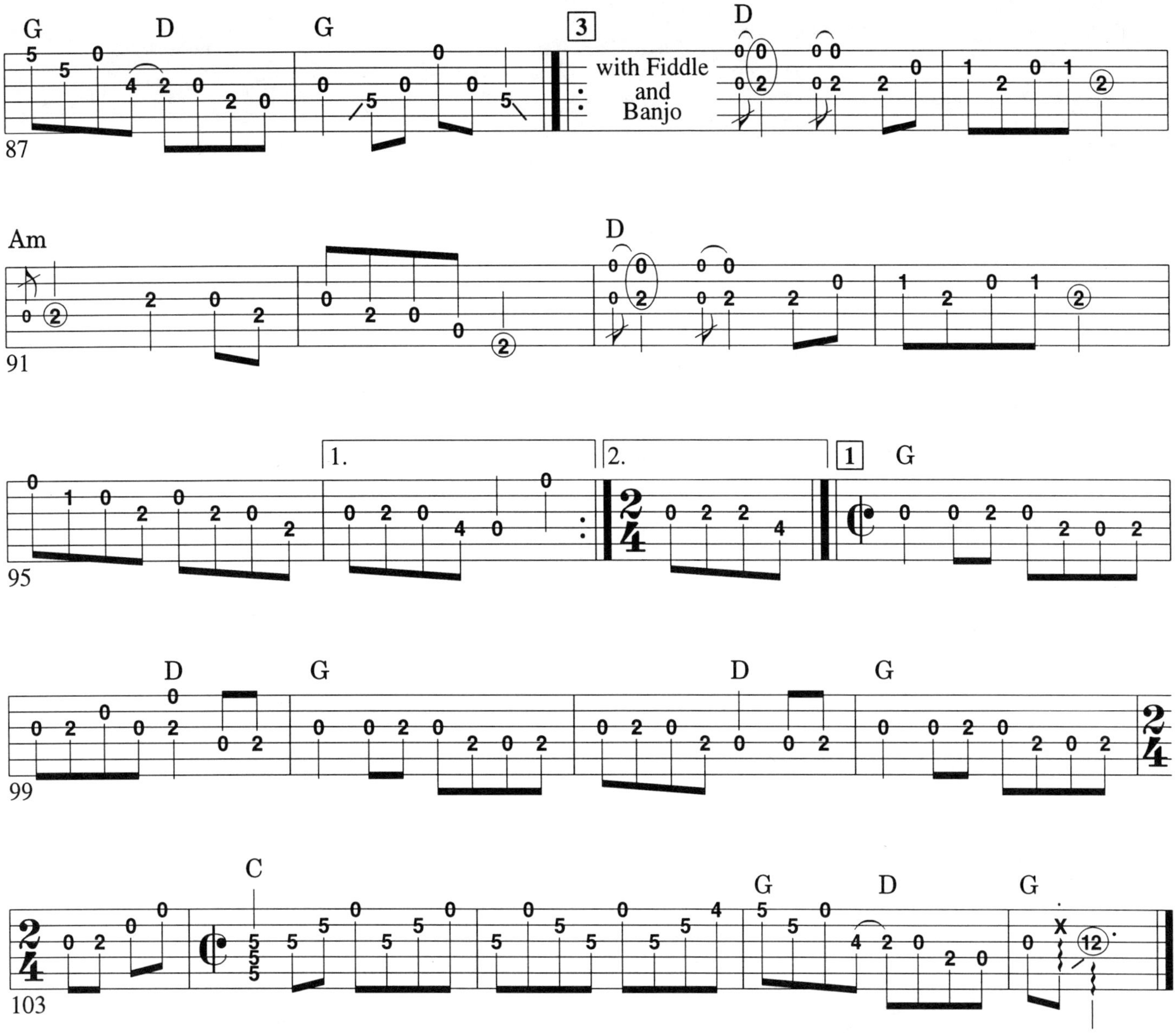
with Fiddle and Banjo

LITTLE GREEN PILL #2

By **Tut Taylor**

Tut first recorded this on a great album with the Dixie Gentlemen in the mid '60s, therefore the "#2." He is the only guy I know who uses a flat pick on a steel guitar. I bought my DOBRO® from him by mail many years ago, sight unseen and sound unheard. I am a satisfied customer.

Before the fiddle and mandolin take over there is much trading of solo passages by Tut and Curtis. This is my best guess as to who is who. Even Curtis was not sure. The exact identity of the licks during the F♯7-E-D chord progressions were beyond my powers of discernment.

After the mandolin solo both Tut and Curtis let fly. I immediately gave up trying to decode their efforts, but Curtis kindly consented to try to untangle the licks. He was there, so I trust his transcription.

Curtis Burch, Courtney Johson and Sam Bush in the original New Grass Revival (photo: Phil Zimmerman)

LITTLE GREEN PILL #2

As played by
Tut Taylor and Curtis Burch

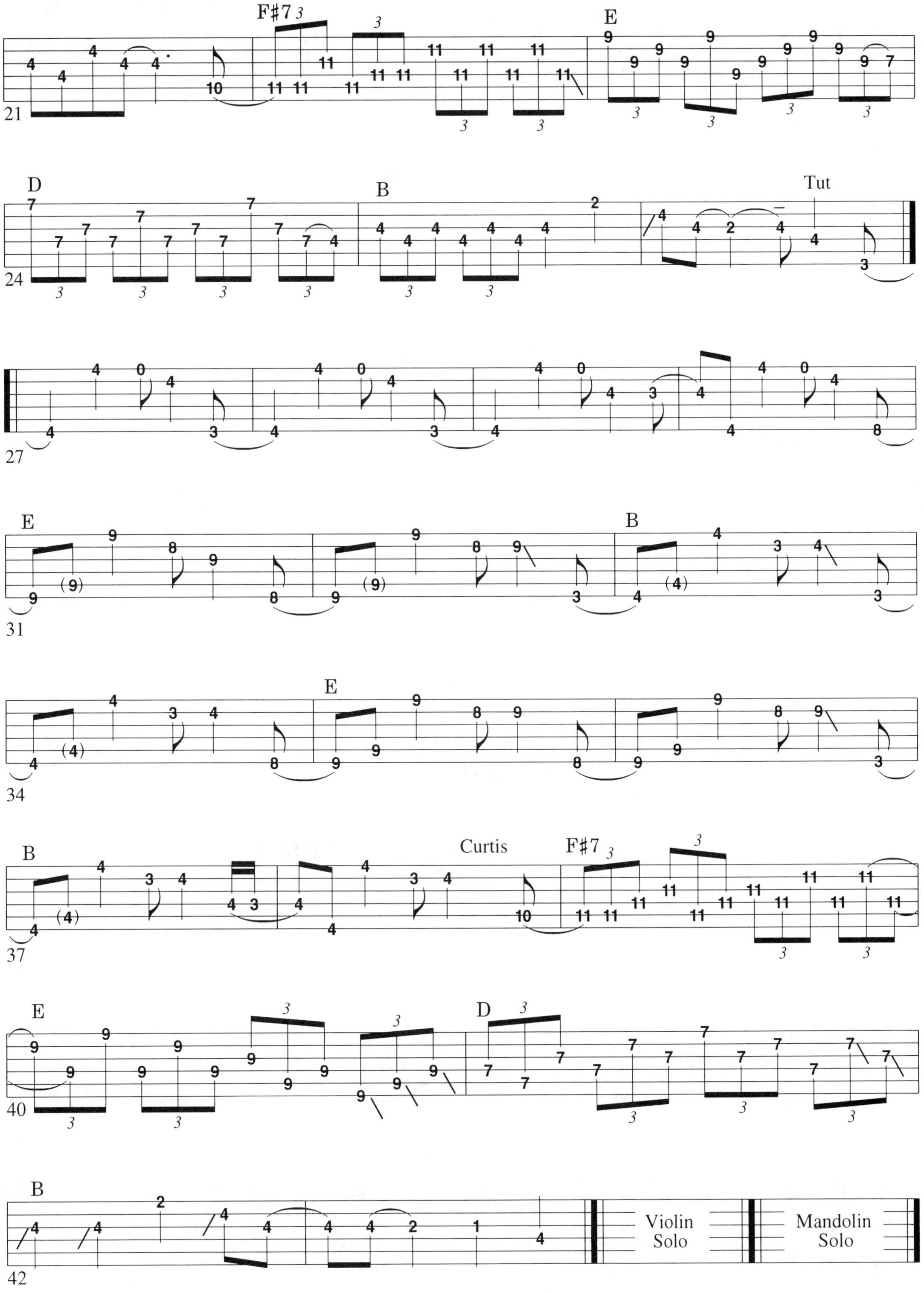
F#7
E
D
B
Tut
E
B
E
B
Curtis
F#7
E
D
B
Violin Solo
Mandolin Solo

Tut
B
Curtis
46
49
52
E
55

B
58
F♯7
E
61
D
B
B
F♯
64
E
D
B
A
B
68

FLATT LONESOME

Words and Music by **Lester Flatt** and **Burkett H. Graves**

This tune is named for Graves' old boss, Lester Flatt. He was a great singer and the most relaxed emcee in the world. People would pay just to hear him talk. Anyone out there remember that flexible, loose drawl introducing Uncle Josh?

Many of the arpeggios in this piece are fillers, and not part of the melody per se, e.g. measures 7, 15,19, and 25. In measure 15 the parentheses indicate that the slide starts immediately upon picking. The parentheses in measure 24 are for a ghost note.

The funny looking business delimited by dashed lines, beginning in measure 27 symbolizes a tricky maneuver by Buck. He sets his bar in a reverse slant covering (sort of) the indicated frets on the top three strings. A straight bar cannot quite hit these positions exactly in tune so a generous gob of vibrato is needed. He forward rolls as fast as possible as he slowly makes his way down the neck resulting in a wild sort of tremolo. Here the parentheses indicate the approximate location of the bar at the indicated beats. The second time he hits this lick he rolls a bit slower.

Beginning in measure 43 I have not notated some arpeggiated filler licks. He does similar fills in the same spot in his solo that follows the fine work by his nephew, Tim Graves.

During the latter's solo Buck can be heard playing some backup fills.

Buck begins his second solo with a shivery lick. He makes a long slide up to the fourteenth fret, holds for three beats with a zany fast-as-possible forward roll, then whips down to the second fret for a slow slide to fret 1.

Following the fermata Buck plays rubato, so my timing is very interpretive.

FLATT LONESOME

As played by Buck Graves
and Tim Graves

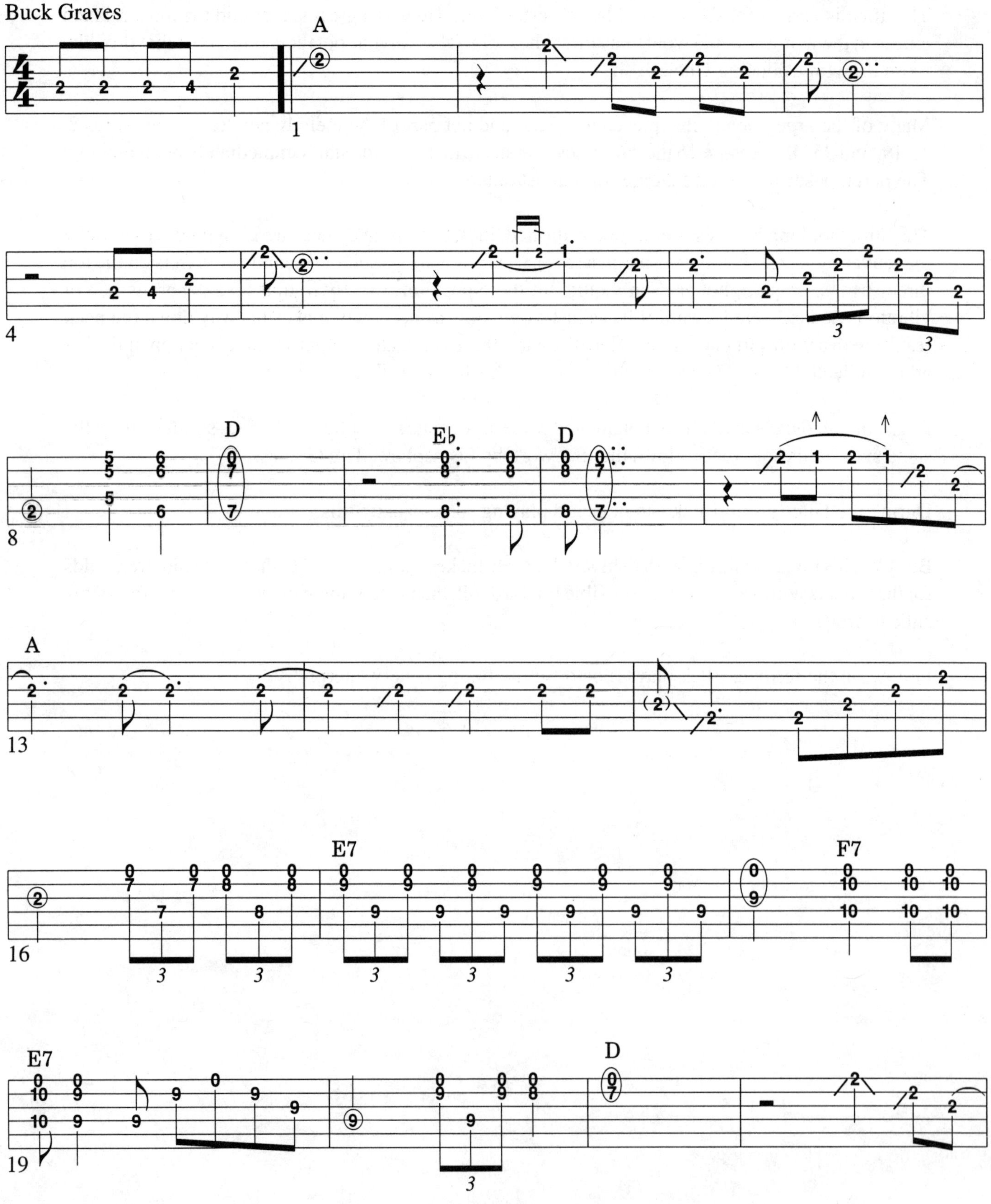

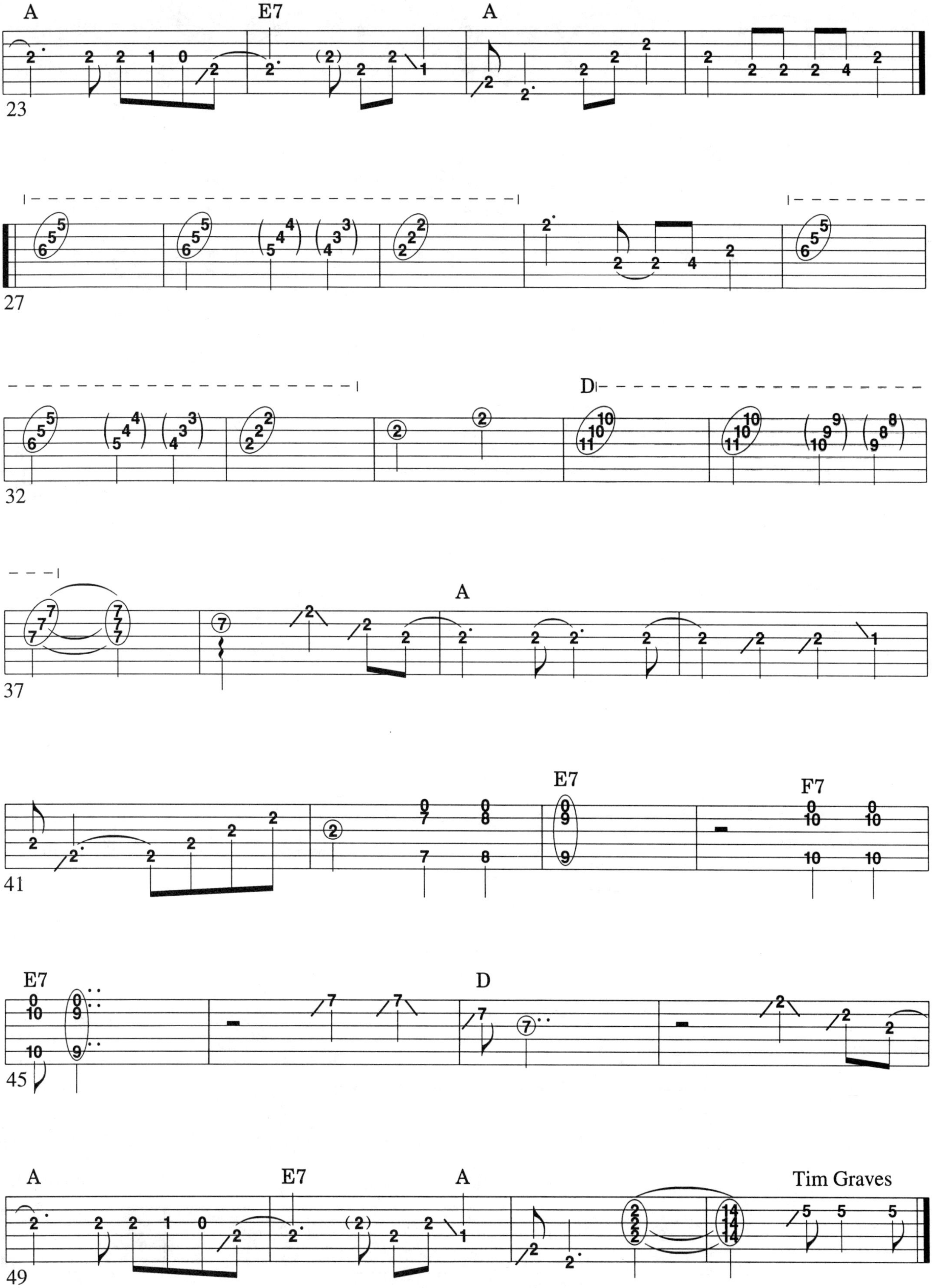
A
E7
A
23
27
32
D
37
A
41
E7
F7
E7
45
D
A
E7
A
Tim Graves
49

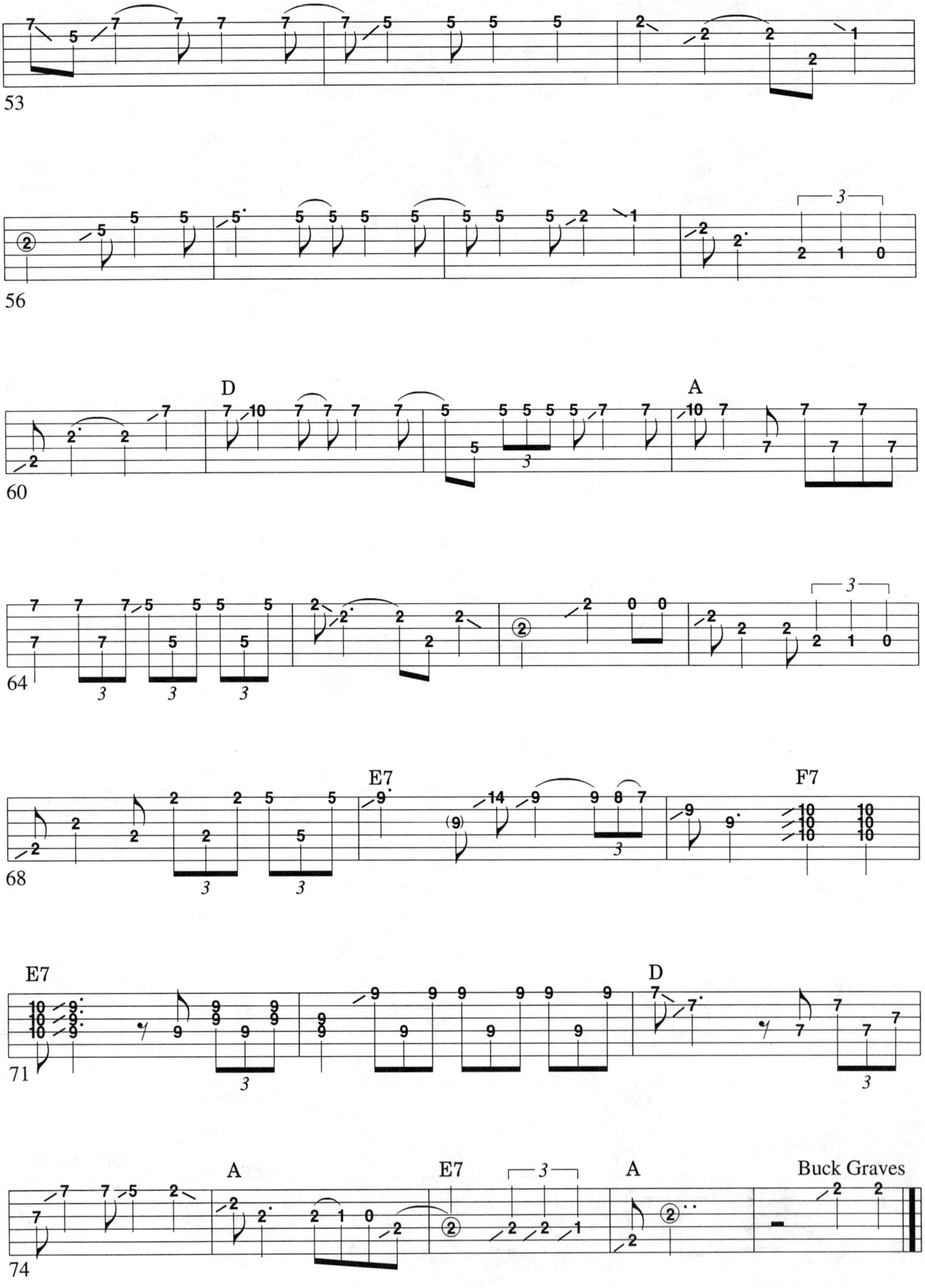
D
A
E7
F7
E7
D
A
E7
A
Buck Graves

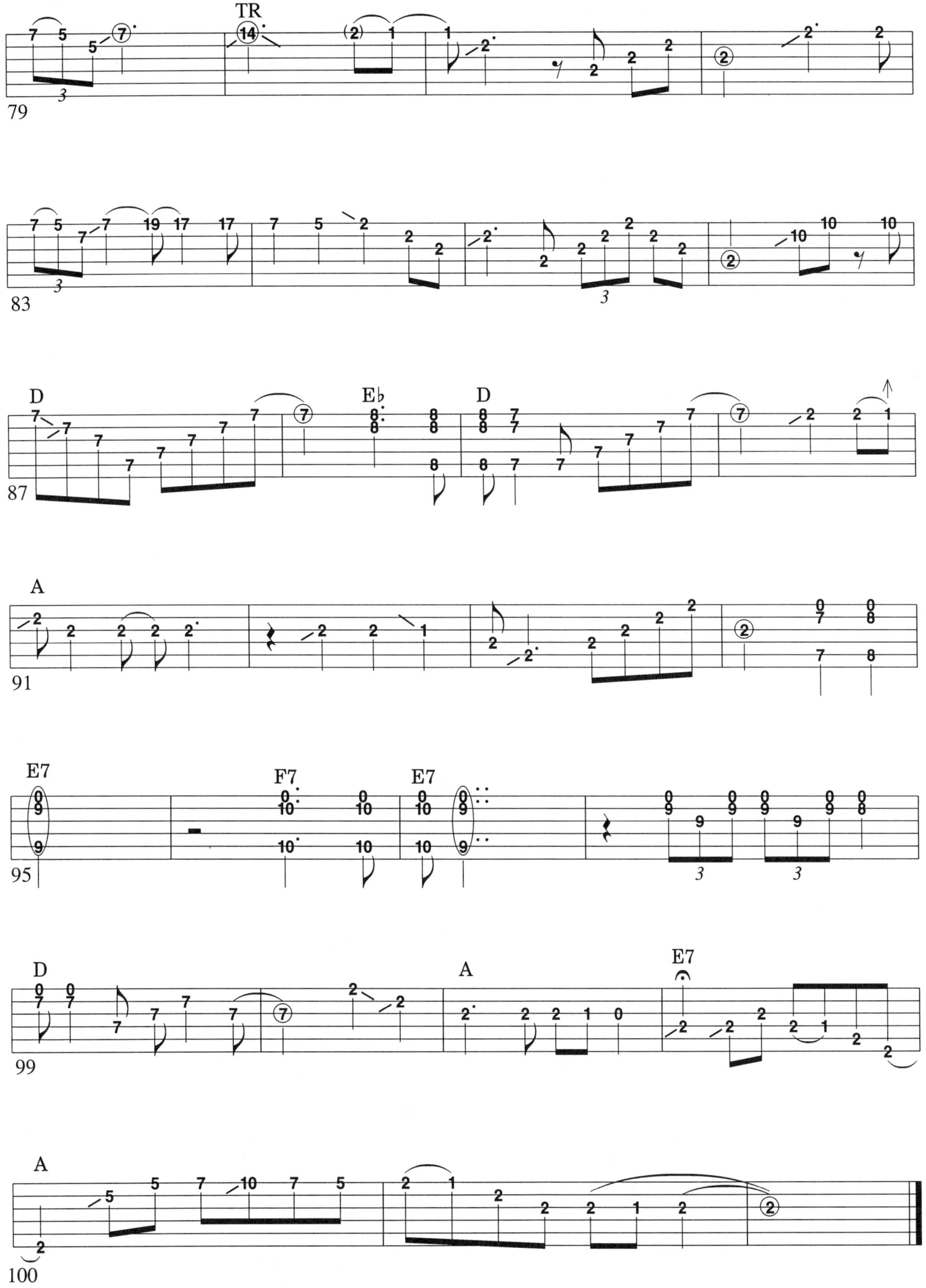
TR
D
E♭
D
A
E7
F7
E7
D
A
E7
A

ABILENE GAL

Since Jerry's introduction is not played in a steady meter I have only indicated the notes he picks without any timing notation. The "dashed" bar lines indicate his pauses. Inasmuch as there is no accompaniment, I have not provided a chord progression.

Section 2 begins with some roll-fillers. The exact mix of open and barred notes is unclear. There are some roll-fillers during the extended notes in section 4 which are not notated, i.e. these notes are not held as long as indicated, but are actually part of rolls. This is also true of the half-note S6-F4 in the last section 2 towards the end of the piece.

This fiddle tune-like piece demonstrates some of Jerry's mastery of the instrument which has made him the most acclaimed acoustic slide guitarist in this galaxy, and deservedly so.

Jerry Douglas (photo: Peter Nash)

ABILENE GAL

As played by Jerry Douglas

INTRODUCTION

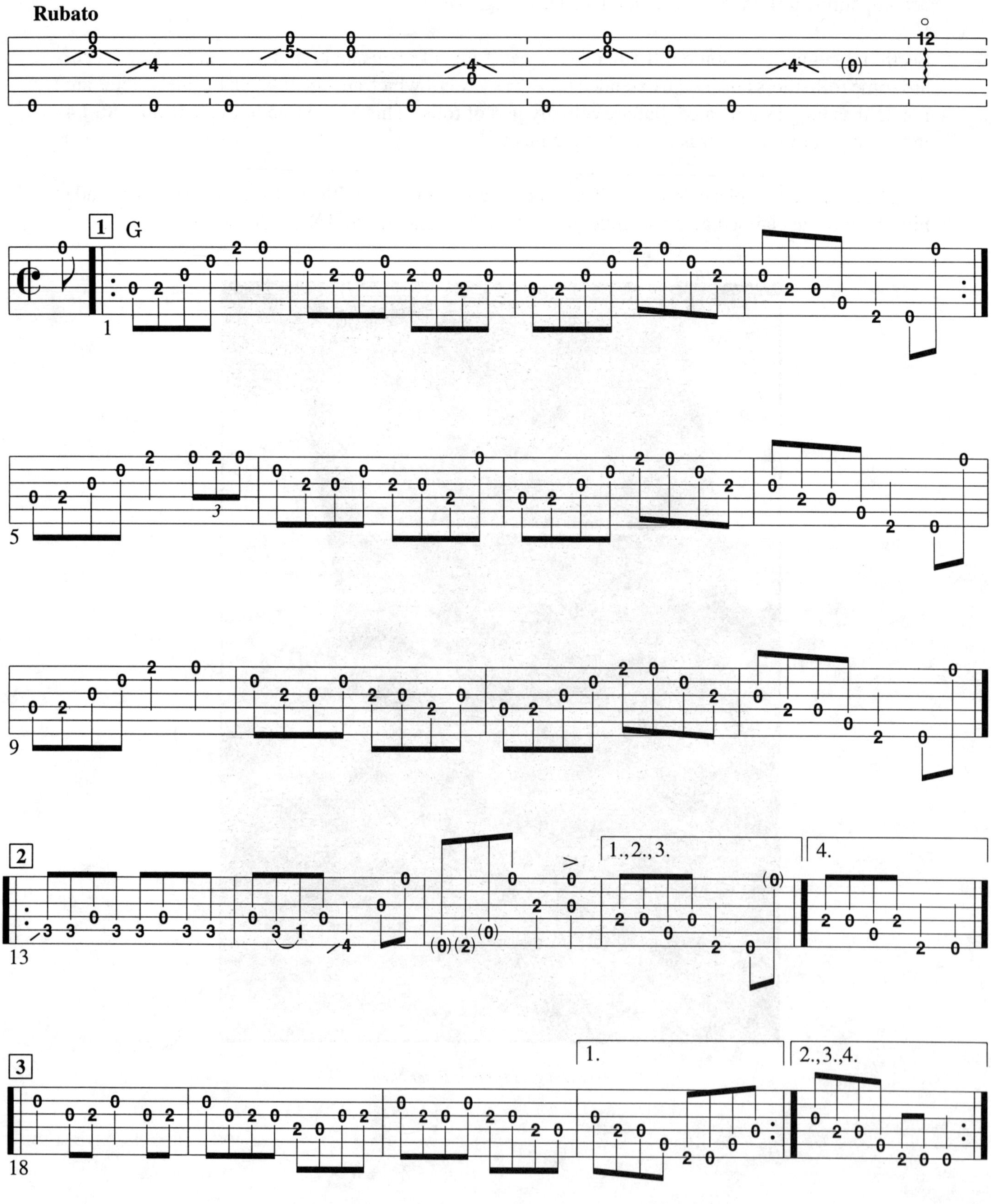

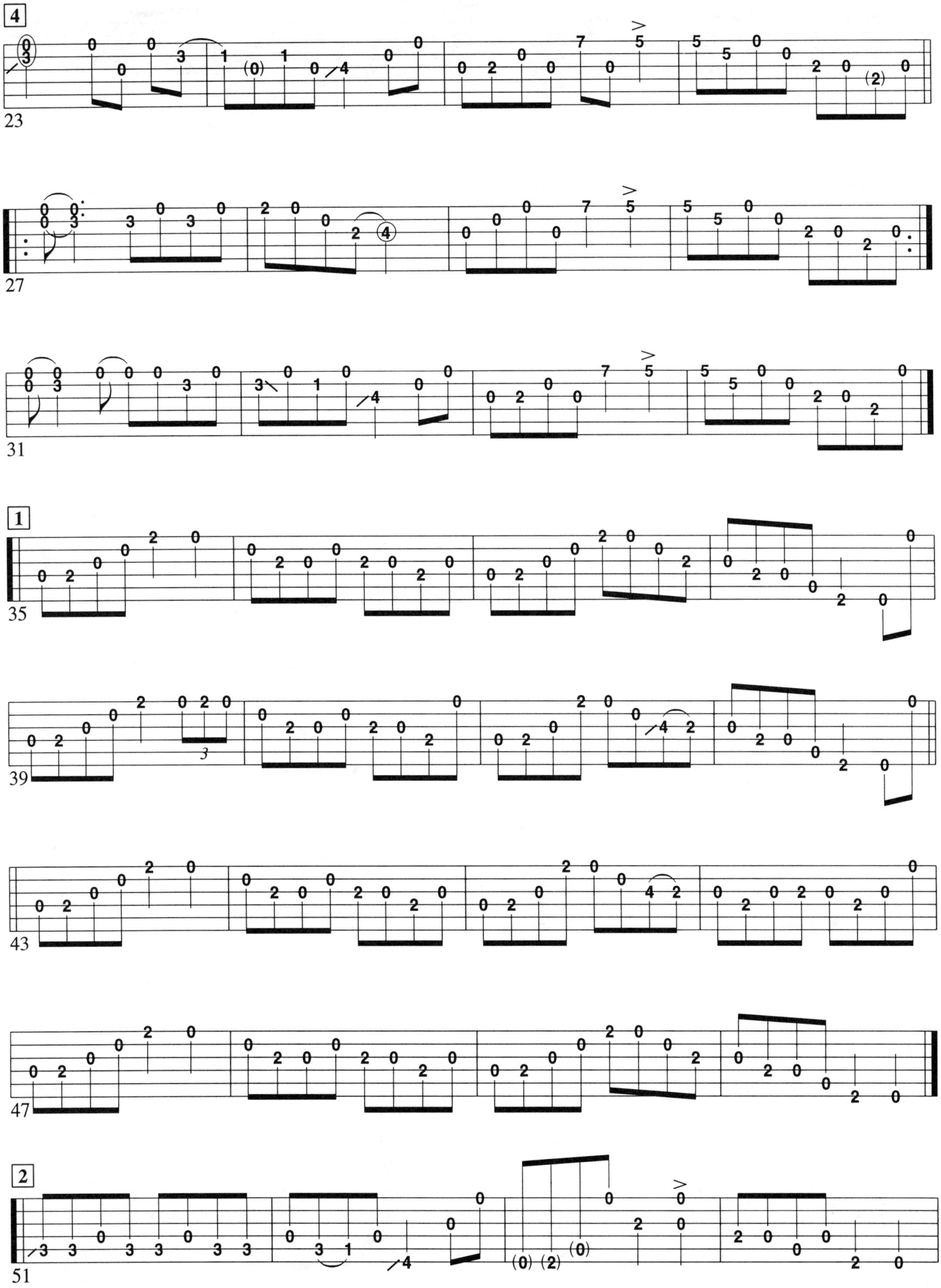
4
23
27
31
1
35
39
43
47
2
51

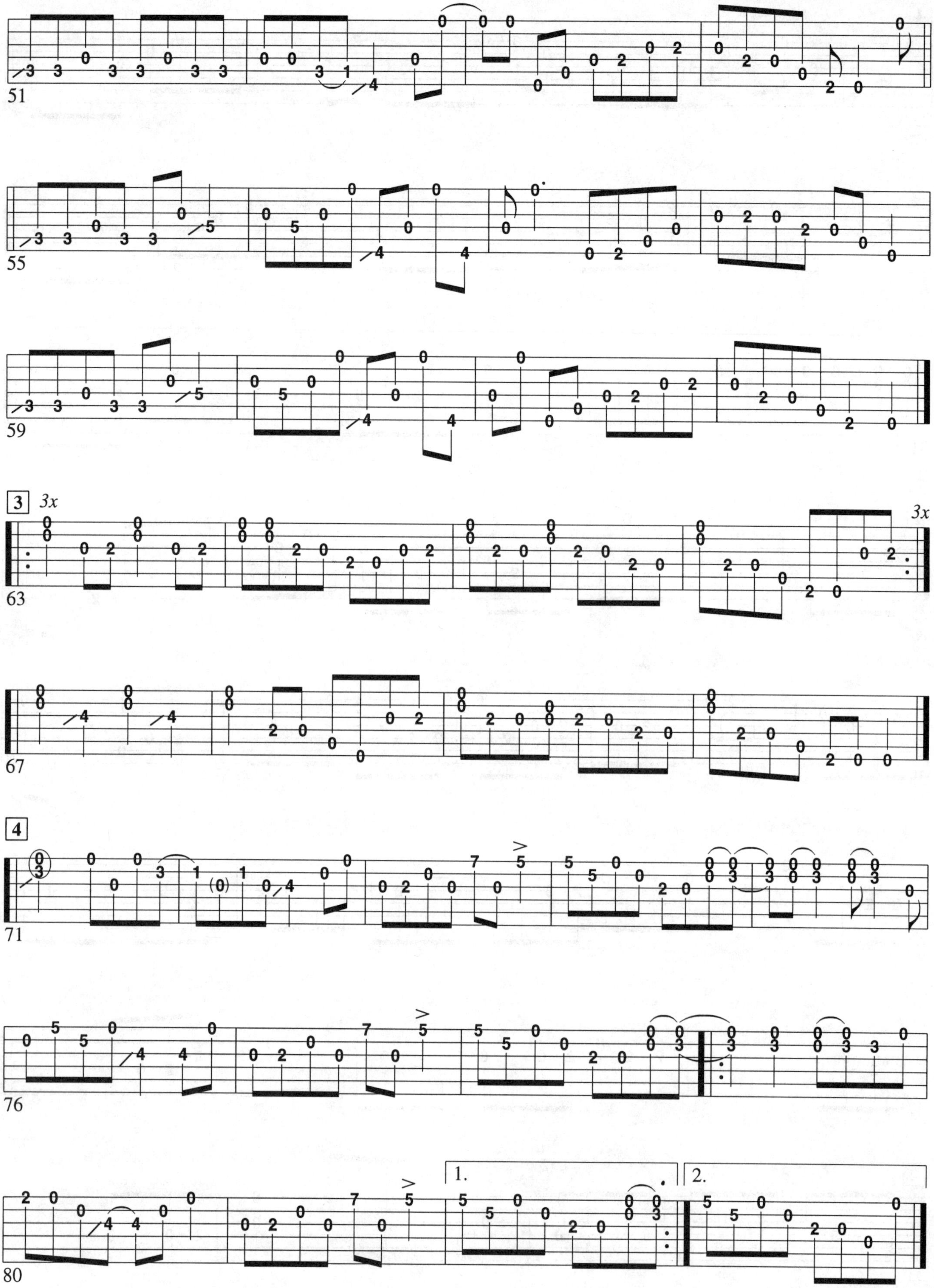
51
55
59
3
3x
63
3x
67
4
71
76
80
1.
2.

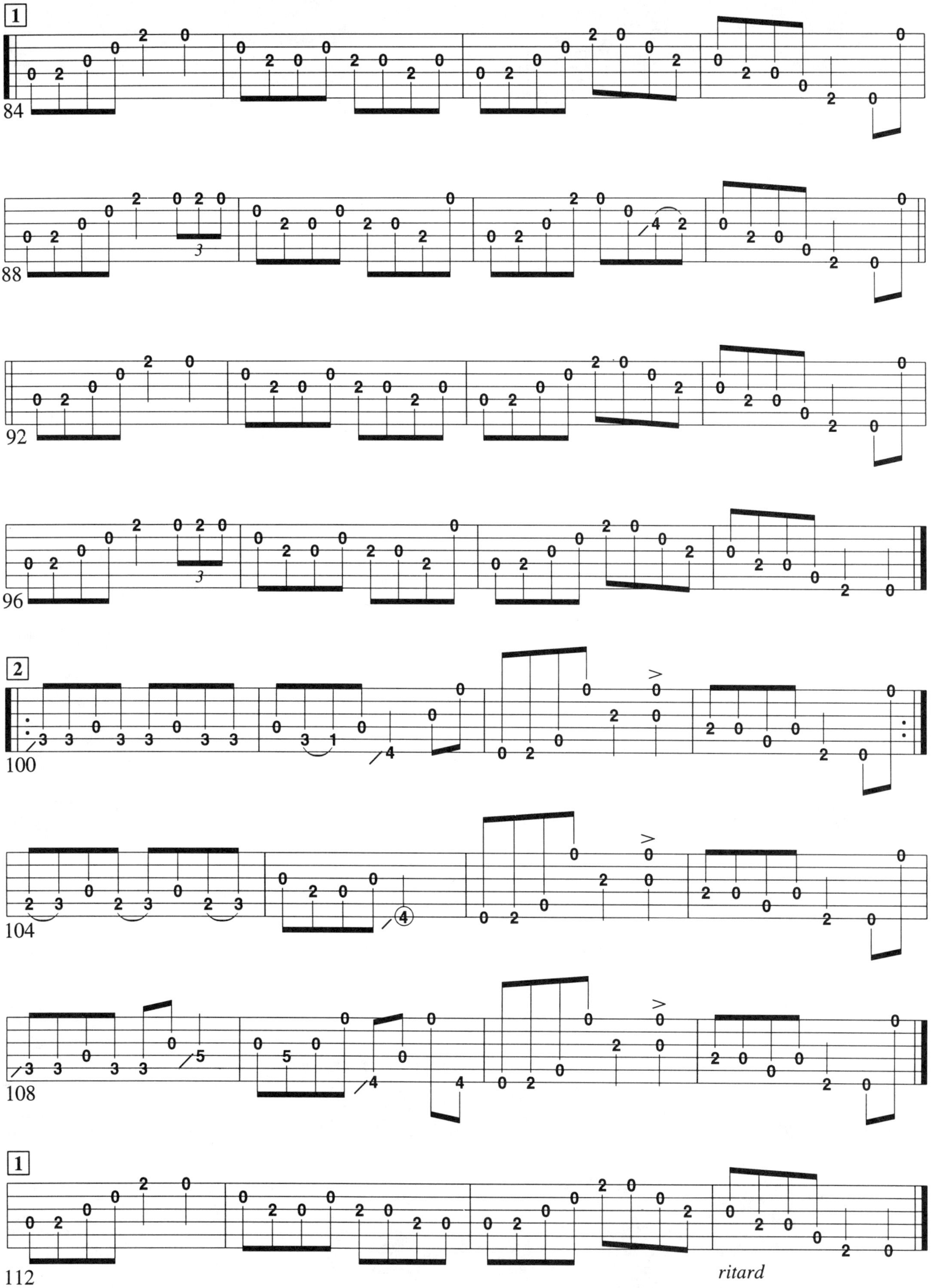
1
84
88
92
96
2
100
104
108
1
112
ritard

McHATTIE'S WALTZ

By **Kenny Baker**

Rob exhibits his pretty playing on this waltz he learned from fiddler Kenny Baker. He's another convert to Scheerhorn guitars. As usual there is no guarantee that, though I transcribed the correct notes, my choice of fretting is the same as Rob's.

McHATTIE'S WALTZ

As played by Rob Ickes

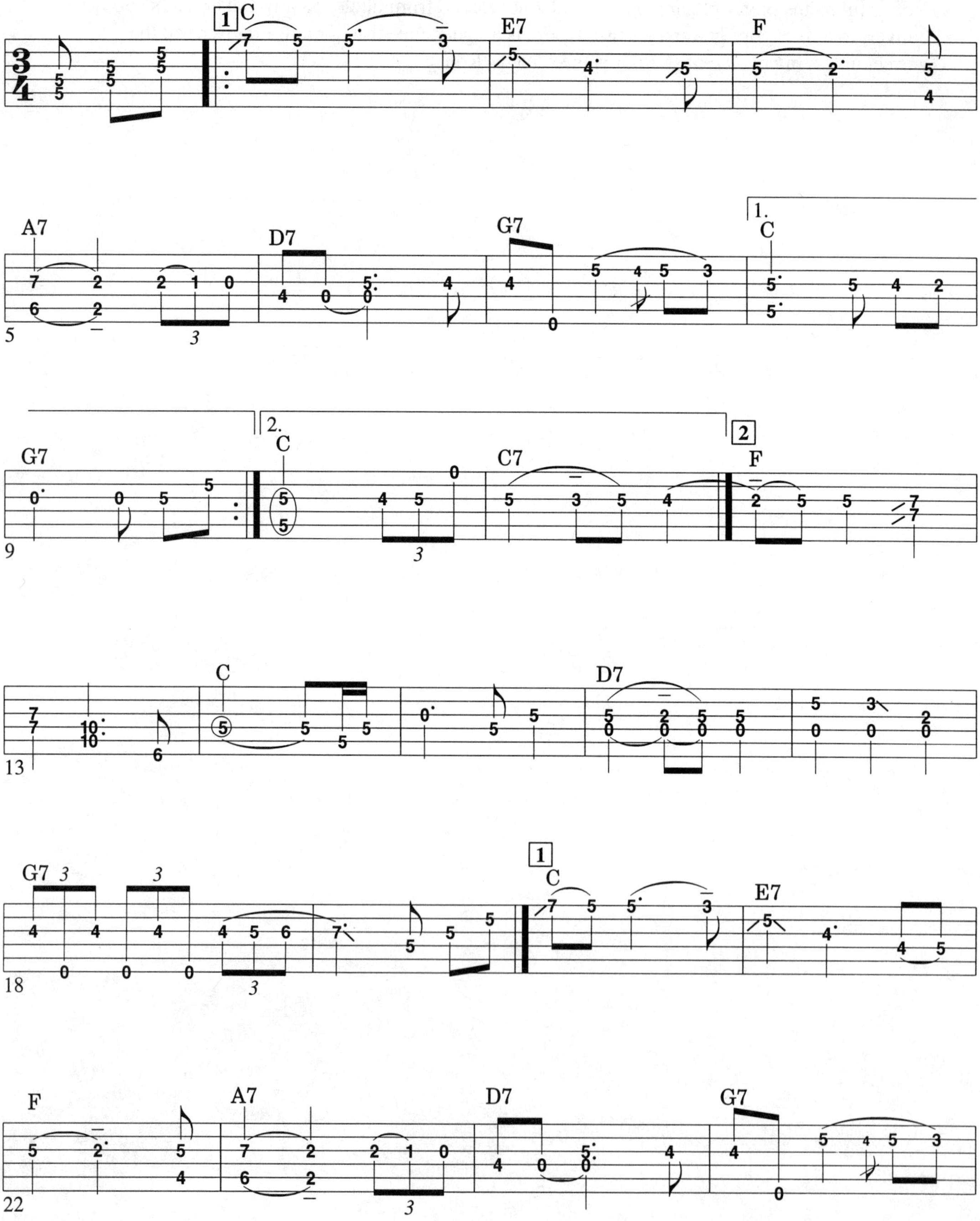

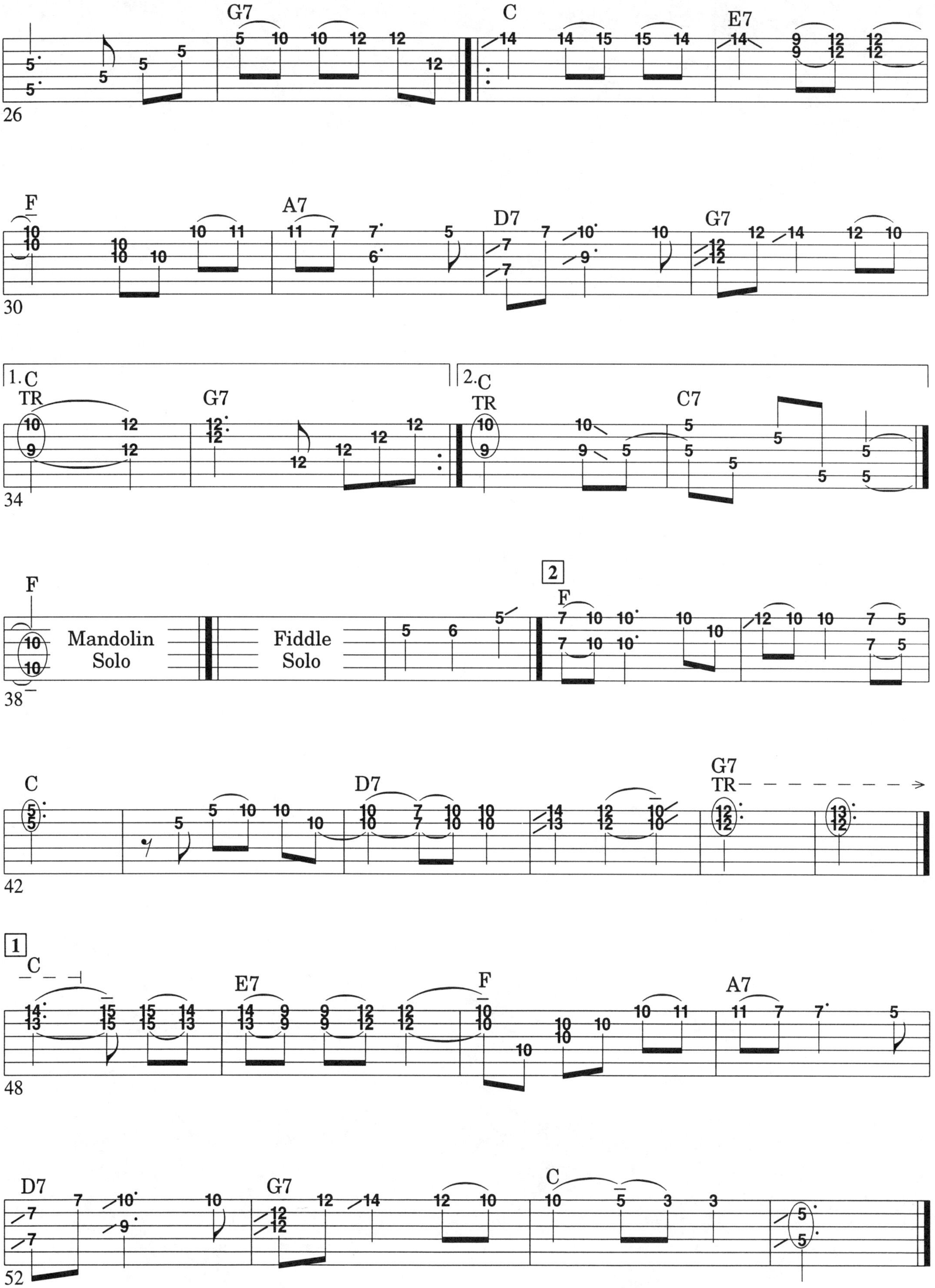
G7
C
E7
F
A7
D7
G7
1. C
TR
G7
2. C
TR
C7
F
Mandolin Solo
Fiddle Solo
2
F
C
D7
G7
TR
1
C
E7
F
A7
D7
G7
C

ACE OF SPADES

I couldn't remember ever playing this tune in quite this manner. I do recollect that everyone liked the tempo quite a bit faster than I could play it.

I learned "Ace of Spades" from Texas-style fiddler Benny Thomasson. It is related to the southeast tune "Little Billy Wilson." In keeping with Benny's approach I made up several variations.

Stacy Phillips

ACE OF SPADES

As played by Stacy Phillips

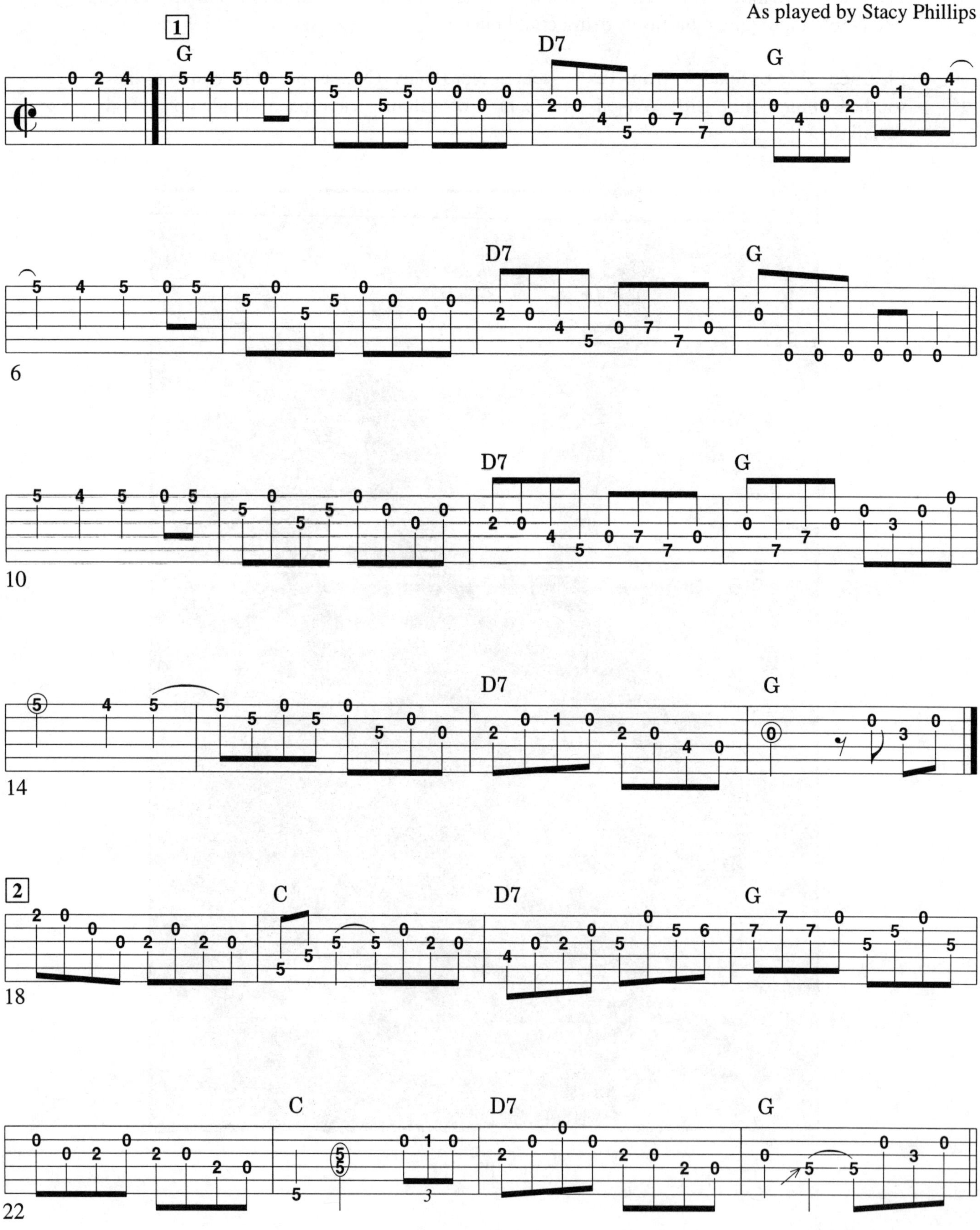

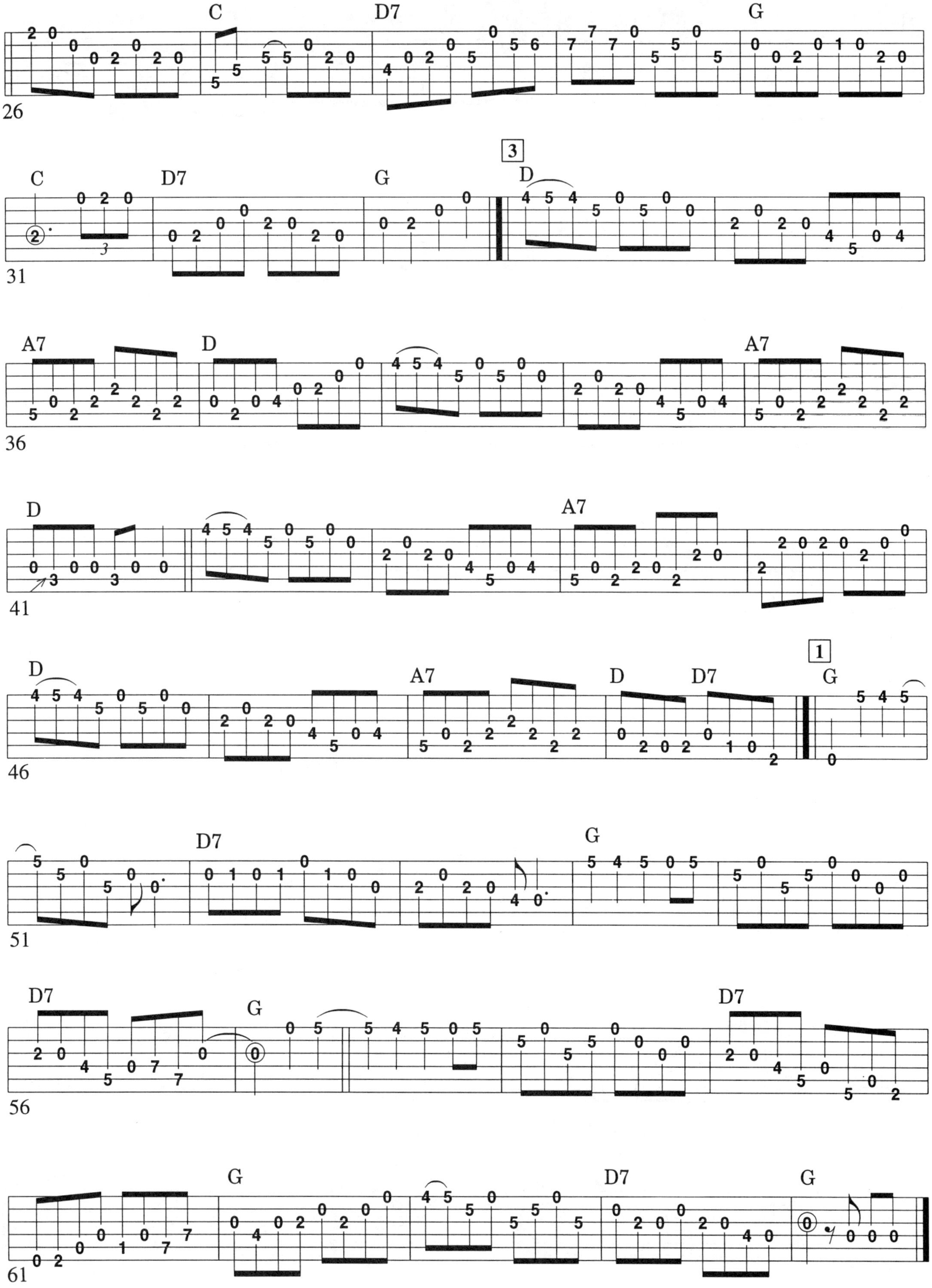

C
D7
G
26
D7
3
D
31
A7
D
36
41
46
1
51
56
61

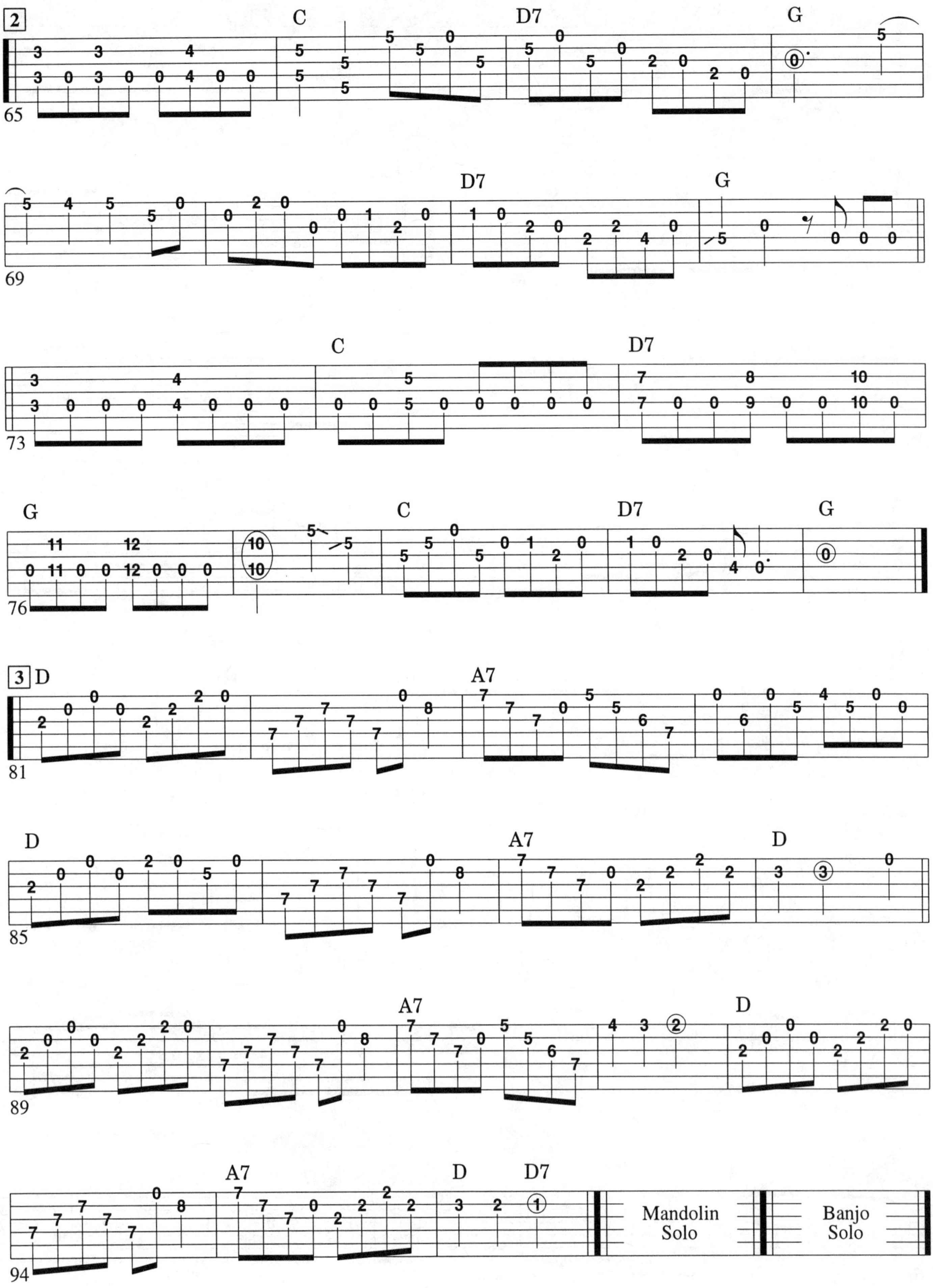
2
C D7 G
D7 G
C D7
G C D7 G
3 D
A7
D A7 D
A7 D
A7 D D7
Mandolin Solo
Banjo Solo

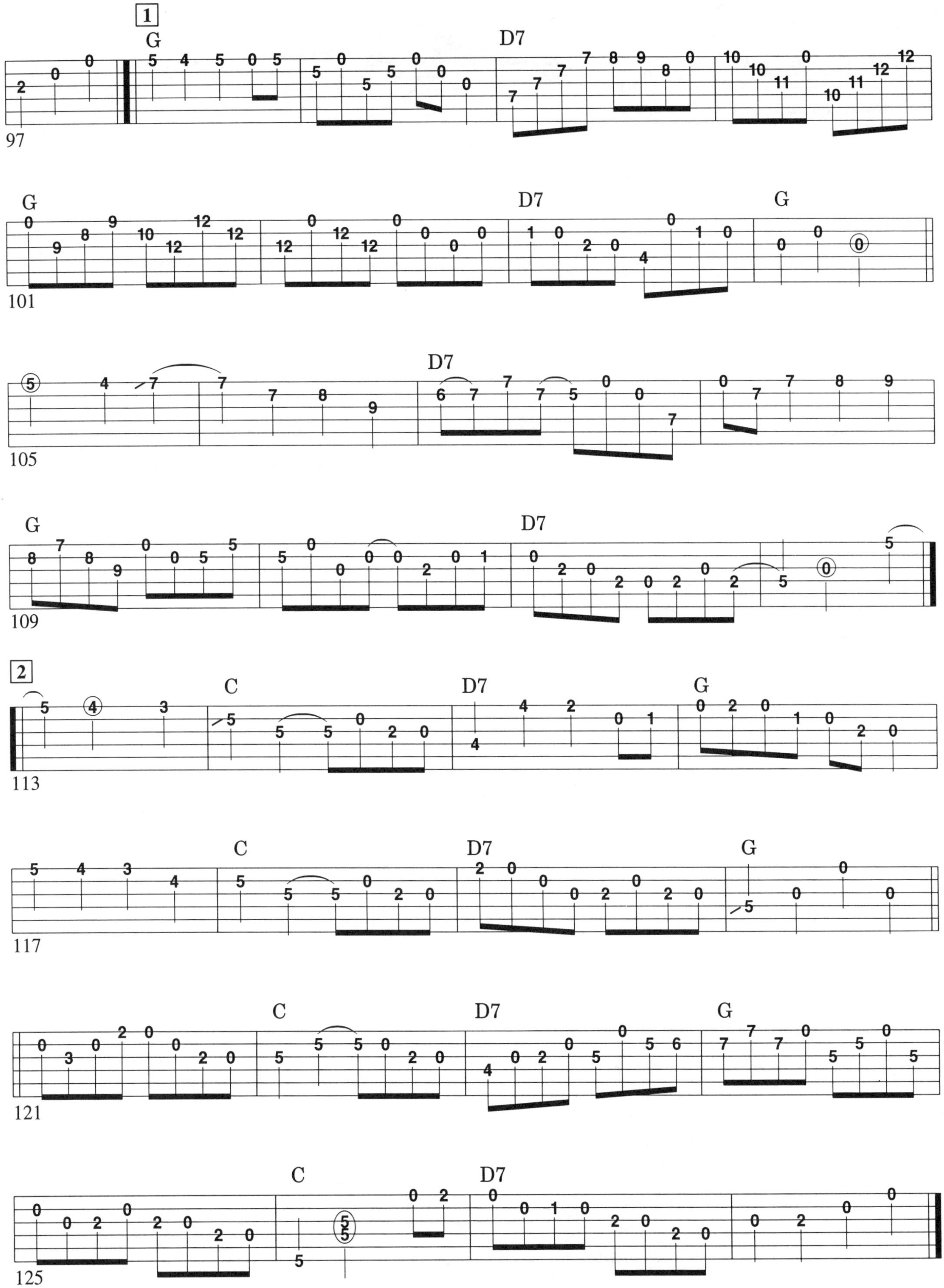
1
G
D7
97
G
D7
G
101
D7
105
G
D7
109
2
C
D7
G
113
C
D7
G
117
C
D7
G
121
C
D7
125

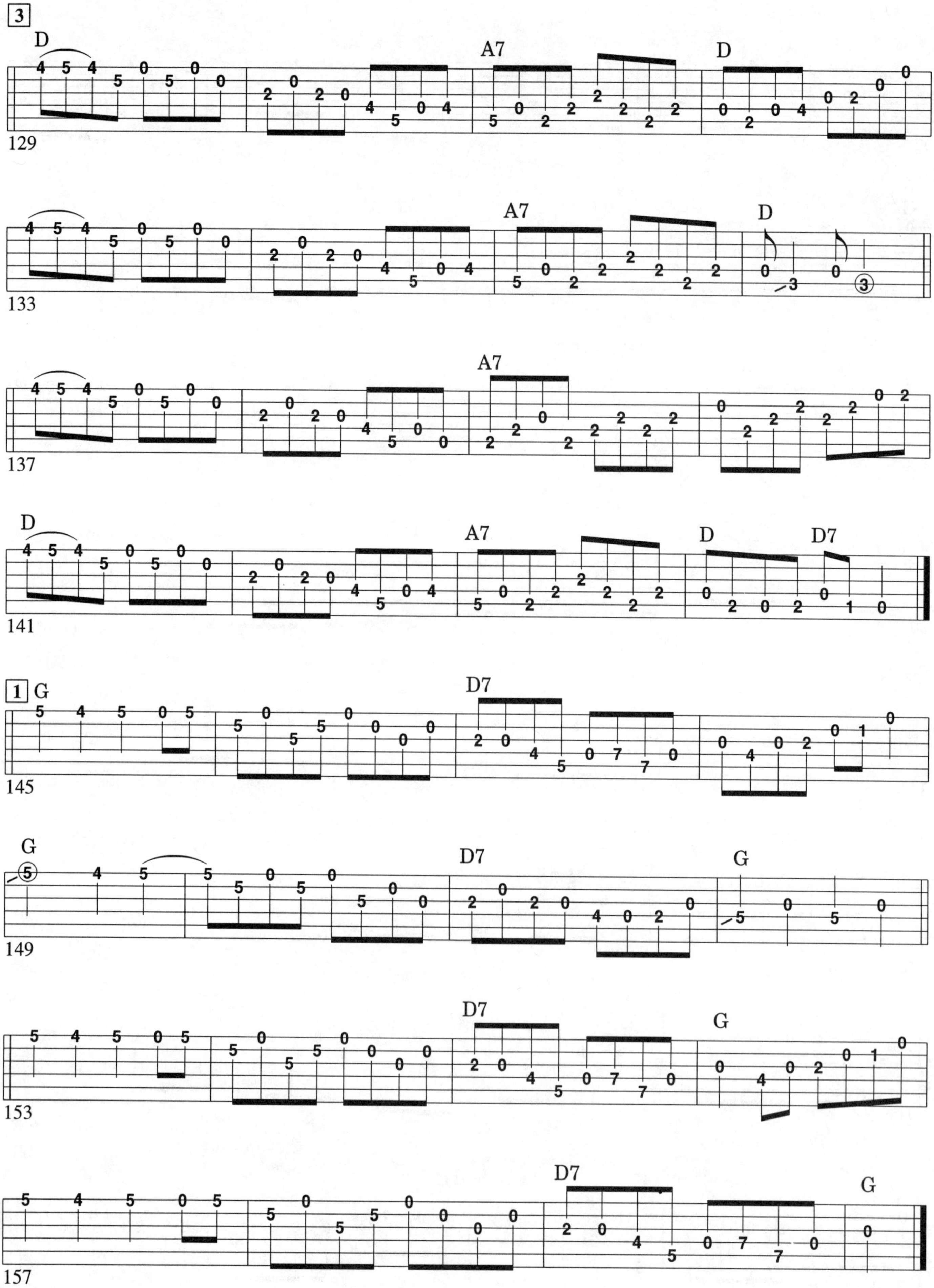
3
D A7 D
129
A7 D
133
A7
137
D A7 D D7
141
1 G D7
145
G D7 G
149
D7 G
153
D7 G
157

SUITCASE

By **Curtis Burch**

Curtis wrote this after his long stint with the New Grass Revival. He helped me out by transcribing these solos. Besides the notated fills, Jerry also plays a few notes during measures 7-10 which I have left out to keep the tablature from being too dense. When they trade, the final notes of their phrases actually overlap the next lick.

On all the two-part harmonies Curtis plays the lead line, tabbed in the top staff, and Jerry harmonizes. On the three-part harmonies Curtis overdubbed a second harmony, the highest pitched line, tabbed on the third staff as indicated.

Read the following before you play this tab!! Curtis and Jerry capo on the second fret. Curtis decided to tab the frets counting from the nut, not the capo, except for the notes that were not fretted. For the latter he notated open strings despite the fact that the pitch sounded was that of the second fret. This is different than the way I approach the same situation. (See "Cherokee Shuffle.")

SUIT CASE

As played by
Curtis Burch and Jerry Douglas

Capo on the second fret

A
F♯m
C♯m
E
26
G
Em
Bm
D
H P
30
F
G
A
34
B9
E
A
38

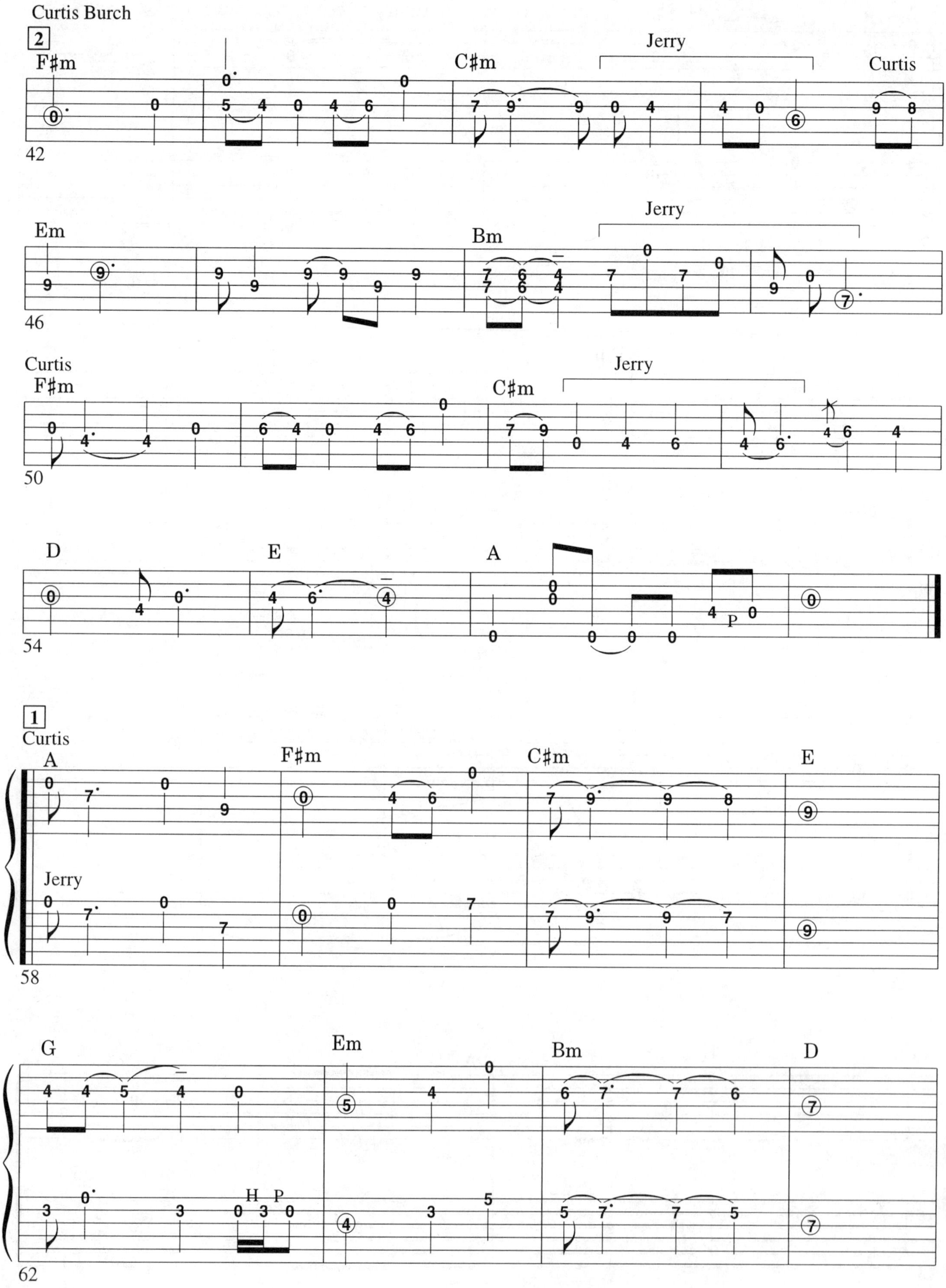
Curtis Burch
2
F♯m
C♯m
Jerry
Curtis
Em
Bm
Jerry
Curtis
F♯m
C♯m
Jerry
D
E
A
1
Curtis
A
F♯m
C♯m
E
Jerry
G
Em
Bm
D
H P

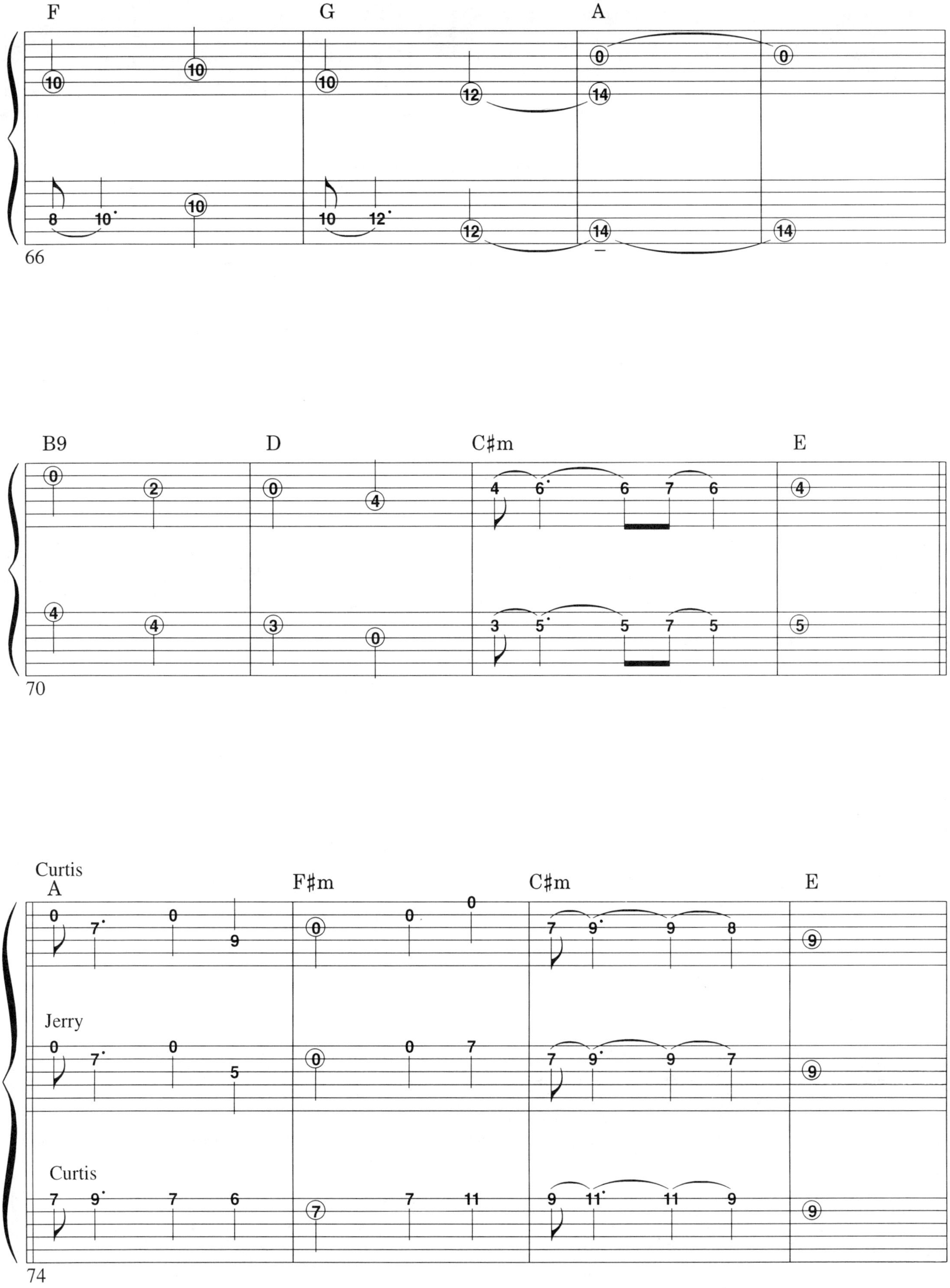
F
G
A
66
B9
D
C♯m
E
70
Curtis
A
F♯m
C♯m
E
Jerry
Curtis
74

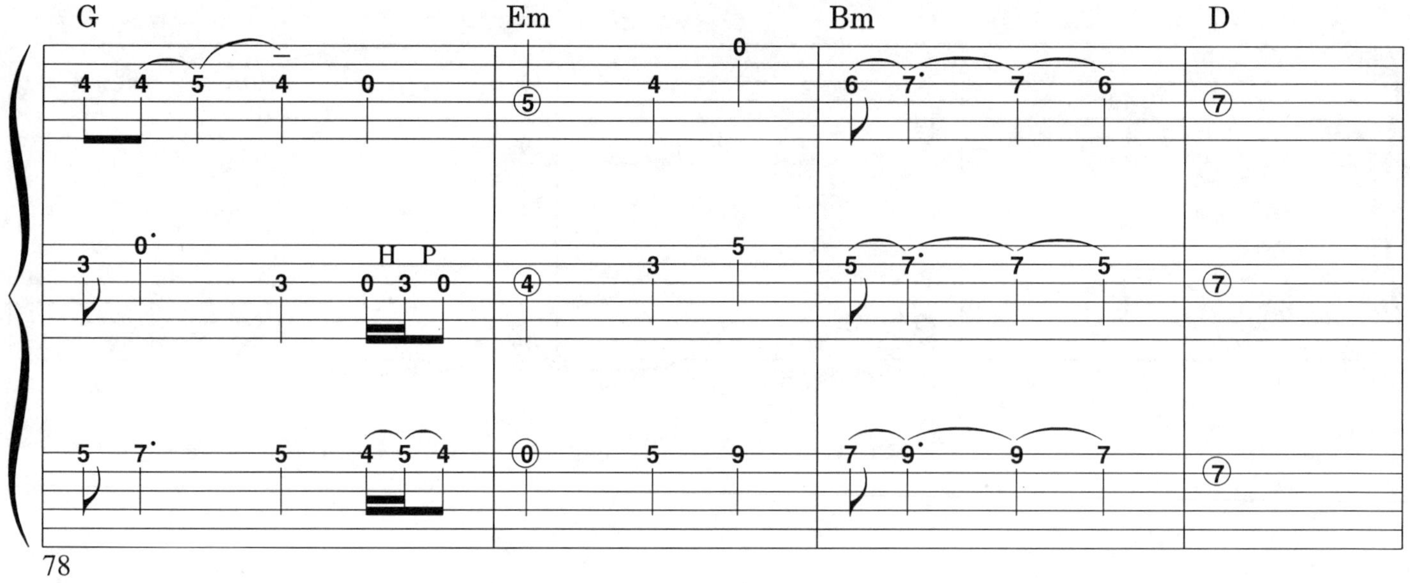
G
Em
Bm
D
H P
78

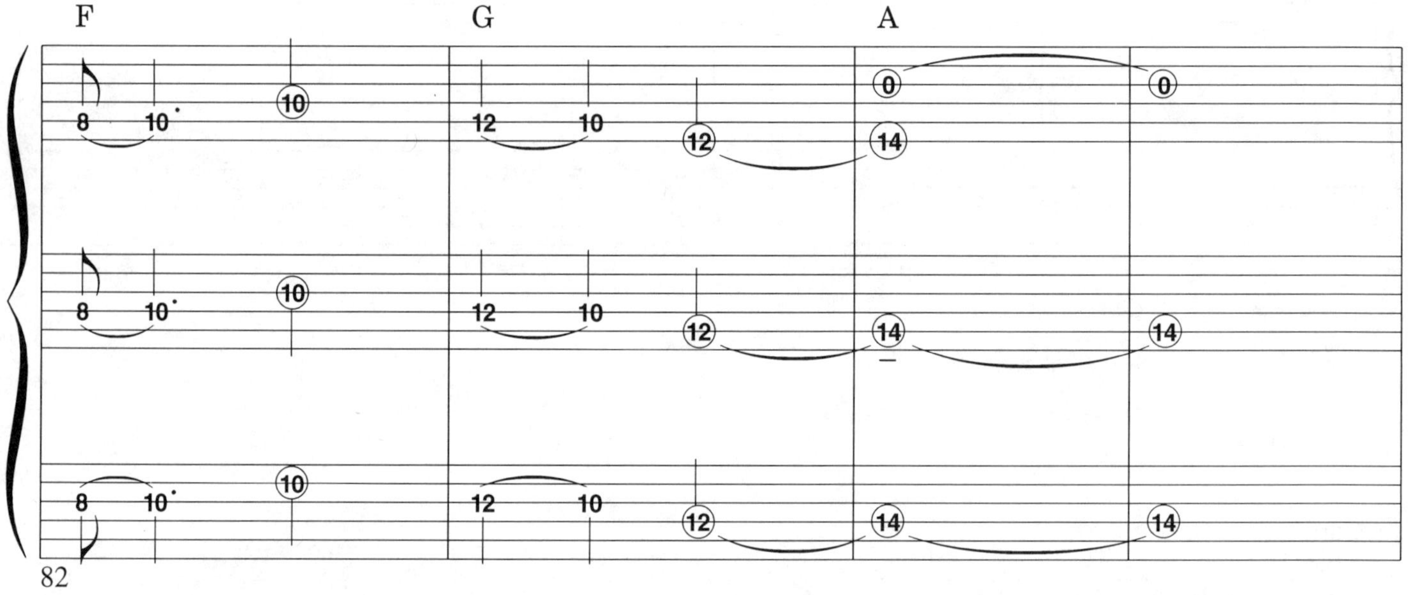
F
G
A
82

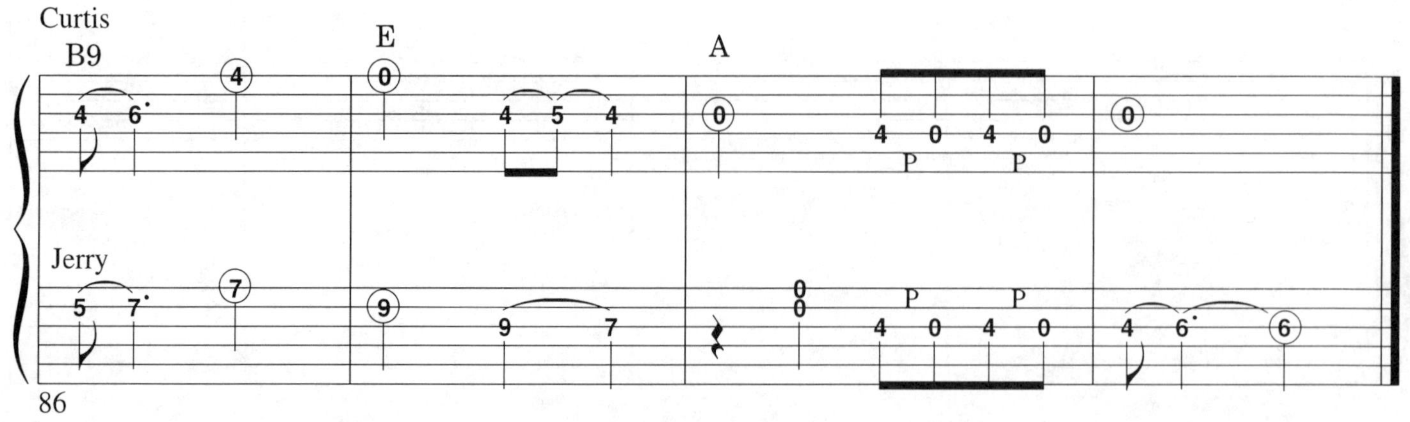
Curtis
B9
E
A
P P
Jerry
P P
86

Curtis Burch
Mandolin
Solo
1
90
A
F♯m
93
C♯m
E
G
Em
97
Bm
D
F
G
101
A
Jerry Douglas
Curtis Burch
B9
D
105
C♯m
E
A
F♯m
109
C♯m
E
G
Em
Bm
D
115
F
G
A
119
B9
E
A
Jerry

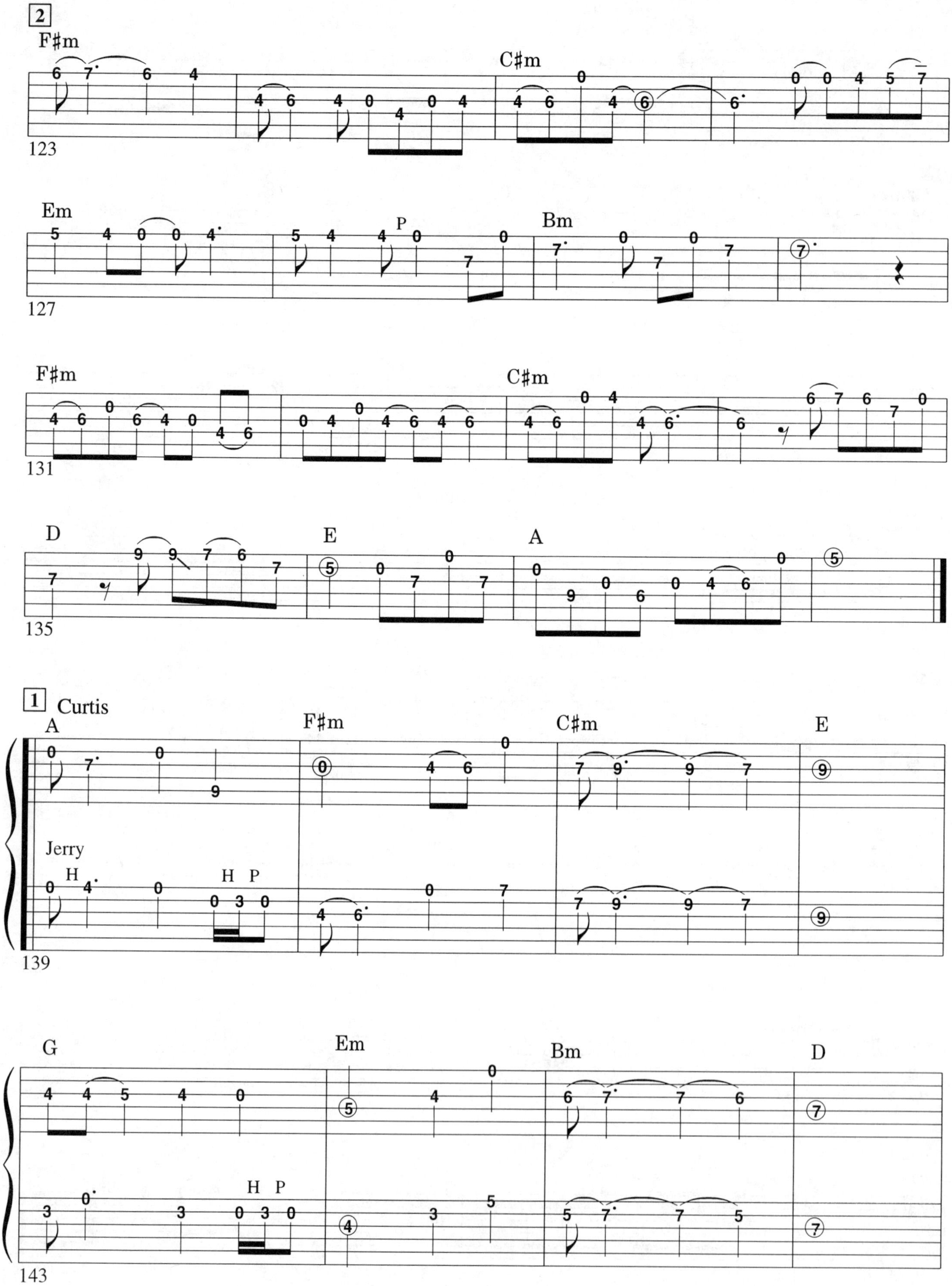
2
F♯m
C♯m
123
Em
P
Bm
127
F♯m
C♯m
131
D
E
A
135
1
Curtis
A
F♯m
C♯m
E
Jerry
H
H P
139
G
Em
Bm
D
H P
143

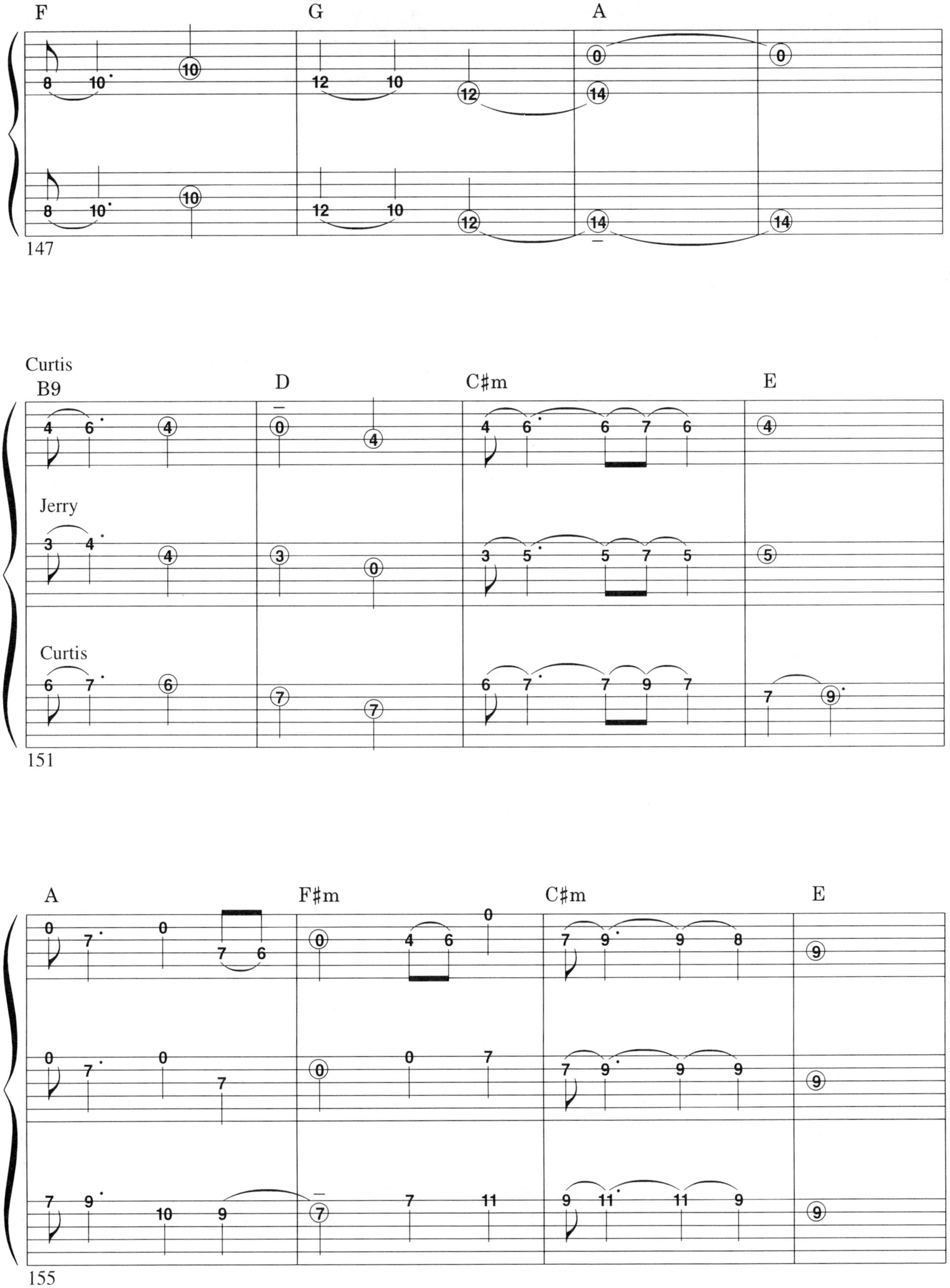
F
G
A
147
Curtis
B9
D
C♯m
E
Jerry
Curtis
151
A
F♯m
C♯m
E
155

G
Em
Bm
D
159
Curtis
F
G
A
B9
Jerry
163
E
A
A
168

CHEROKEE SHUFFLE

Sally capoes up two frets to play in this fiddle piece's standard key of A. I have tabbed the music counting from the placement of the capo and have notated the chords as played on the album. For example, what I have tabbed as fret 5 is five frets above the capo and, simultaneously, seven frets above the nut. If you play this without the capo all the notes would come out fine but the chords would transpose down a whole step; A to G, F♯m to Em, D to C, and E7 to D7.

As usual there are some arpeggiated fills that I could not quite capture.

CHEROKEE SHUFFLE

Capo on the second fret

As played by Sally Van Meter

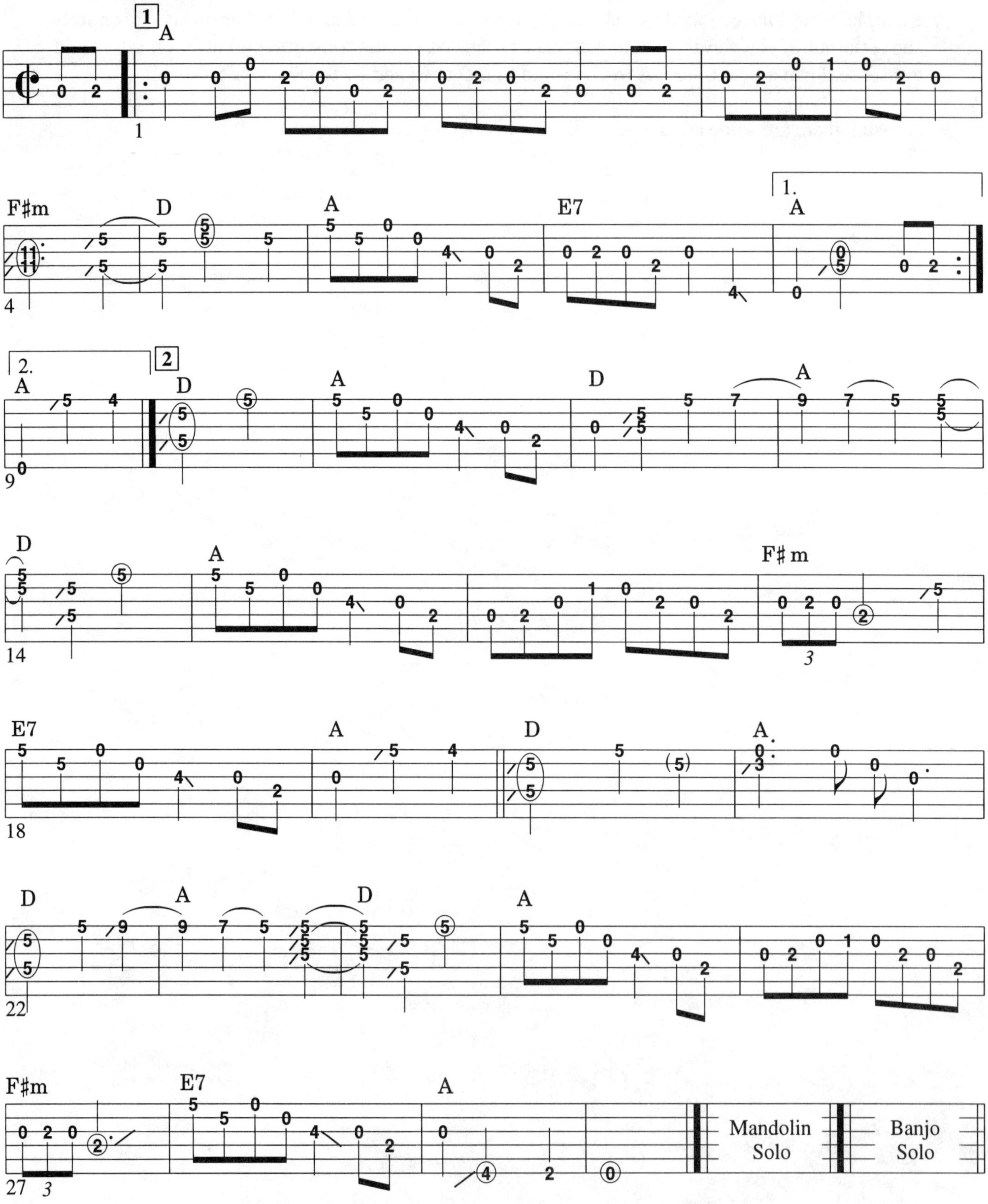

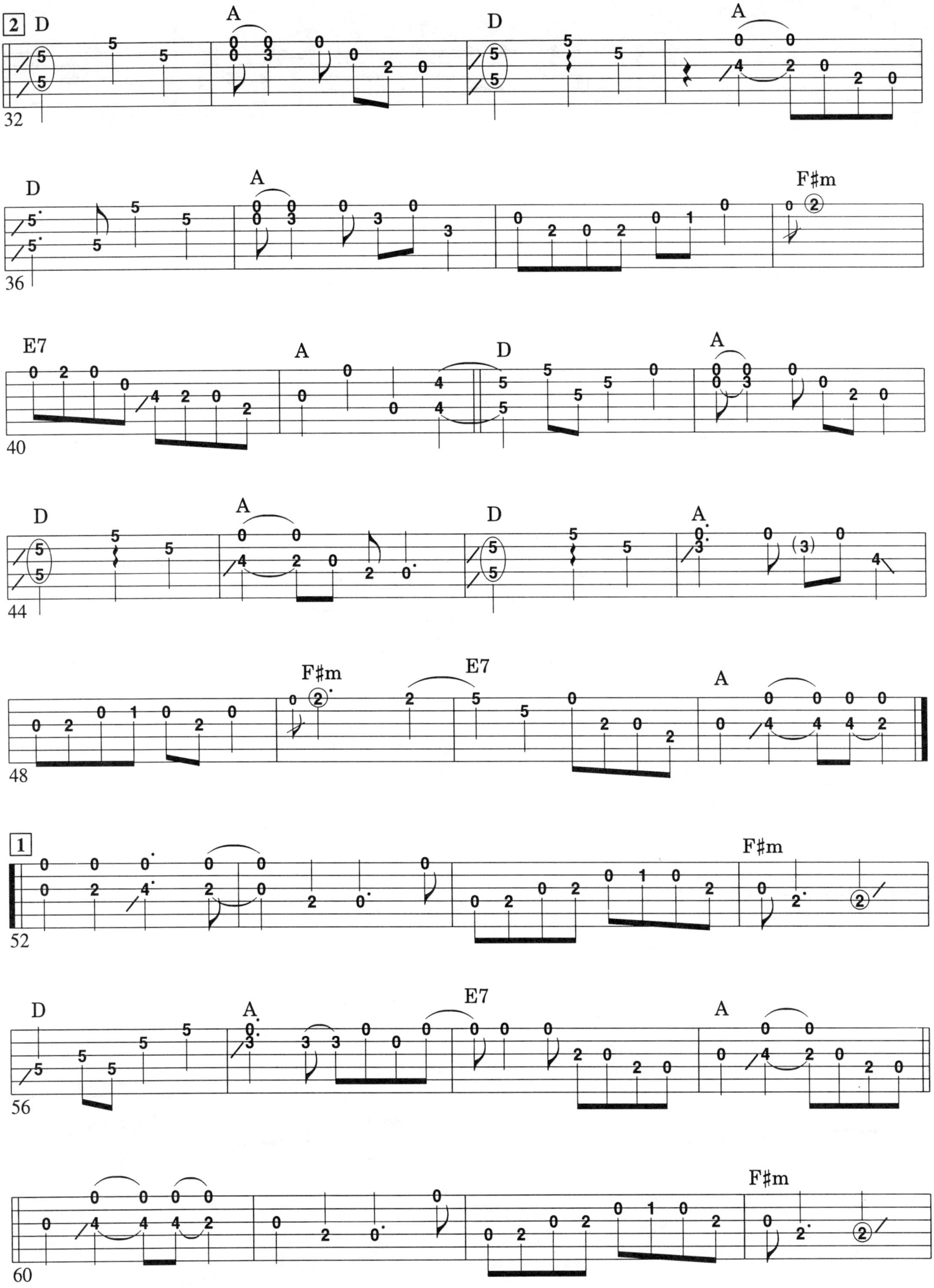
2
D A D A
D A F#m
E7 A D A
D A D A
F#m E7 A
1
F#m
D A E7 A
F#m

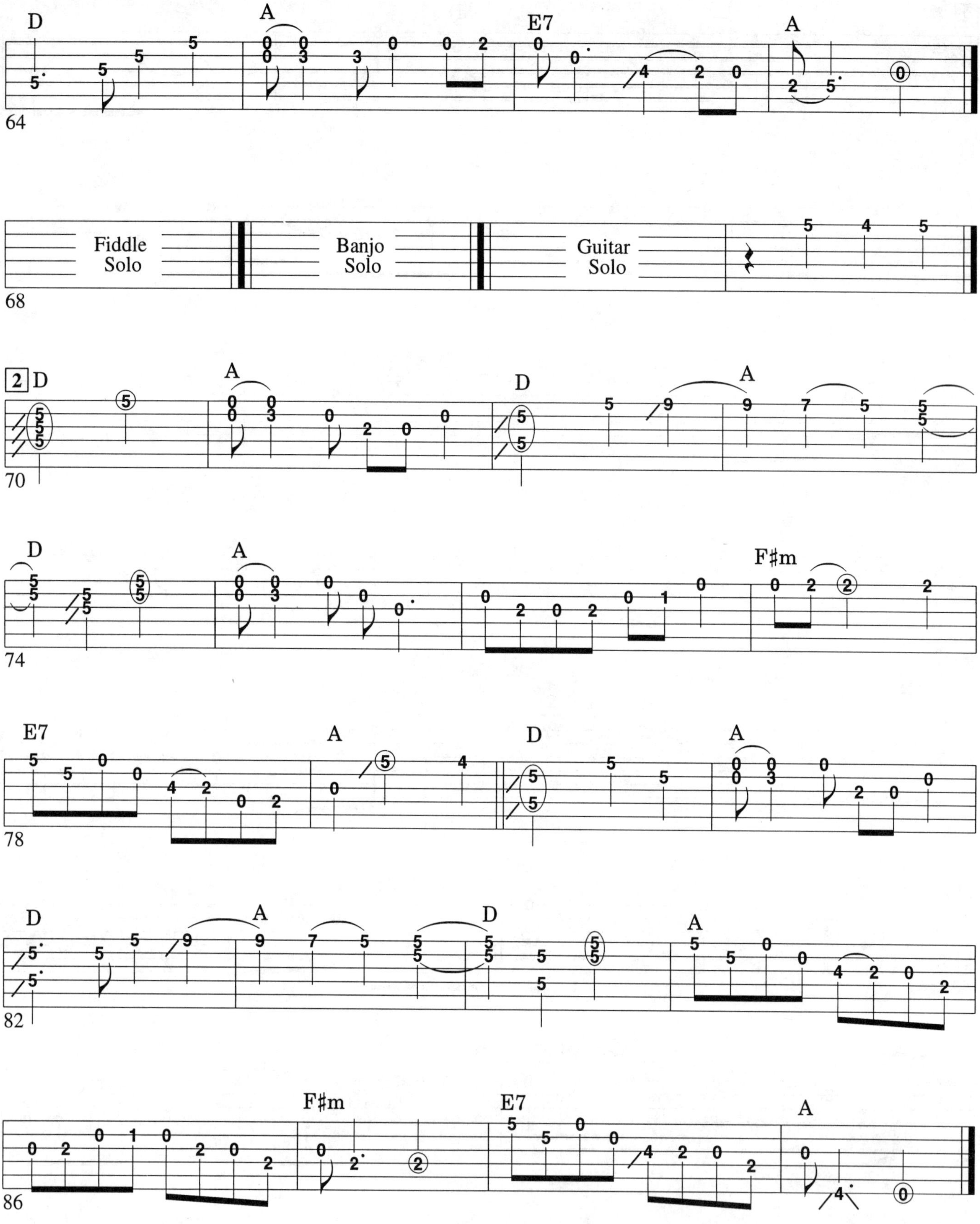
D A E7 A
Fiddle Solo
Banjo Solo
Guitar Solo
D A D A
D A F♯m
E7 A D A
D A D A
F♯m E7 A

LONESOME DOBRO®

By **Tut Taylor**

In measures 31-32 Tut keeps the notes on the first and third strings ringing (i.e. are not damped). Notating all the tie lines would have confused the issue.

Curtis capoes up two frets so it is as if he is playing out of the key of D. I have counted his fretting from the capo as I did in Sally Van Meter's "Cherokee Shuffle."

In measure 34 Curtis hits one third string instead of second during the tremolo. In measure 53 the eccentric notation indicates a tremolo between the thumb on S4-F9 and the index and middle fingers simultaneously picking the second and third strings. He does a similar move in his solo right after the fiddle solo.

During Tut's last whack at the first section Curtis does some backup which I have not tabbed. Tut first recorded this on one of his excellent, but long deleted albums on World Pacific.

LONESOME DOBRO®

As played by
Tut Taylor and Curtis Burch

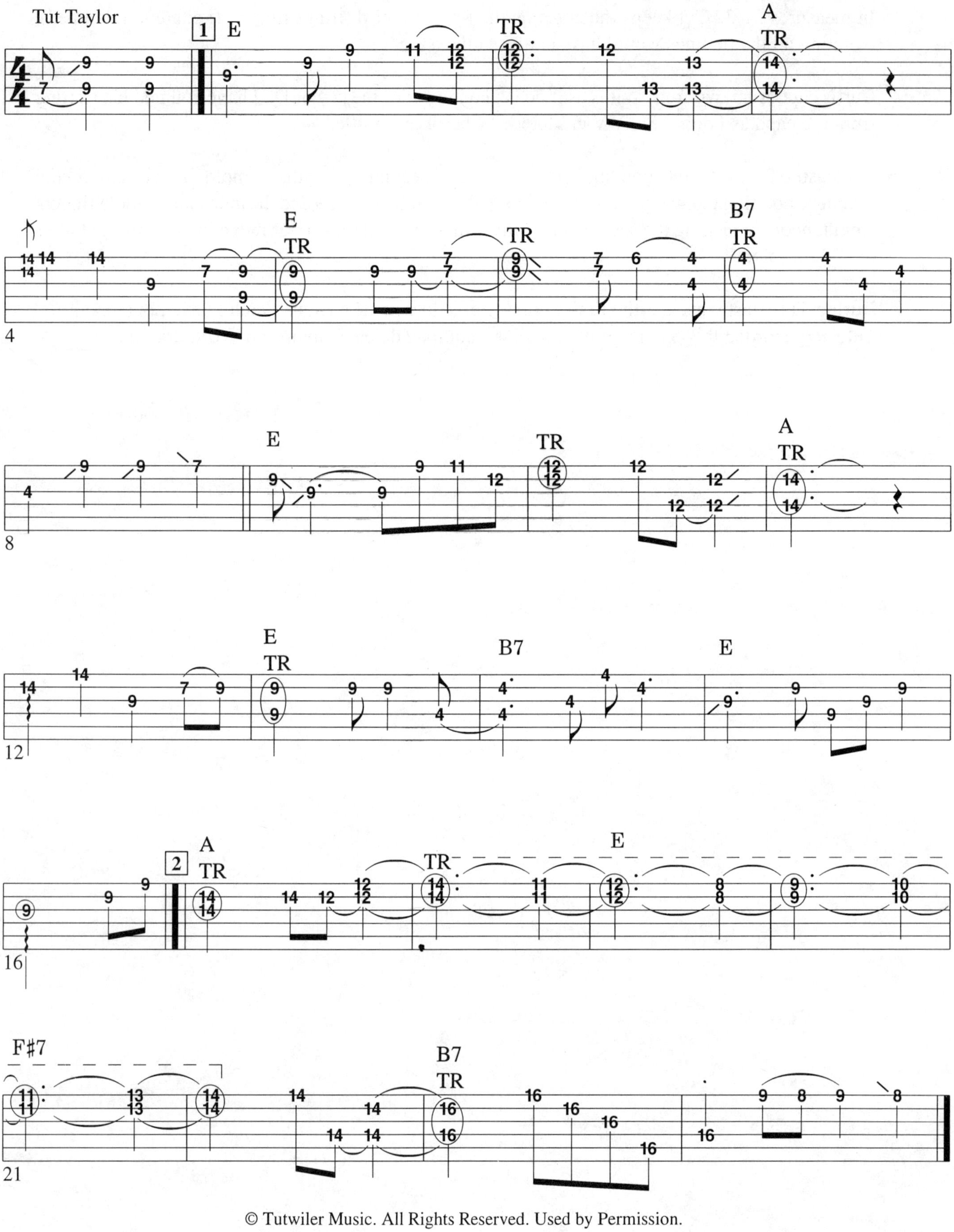

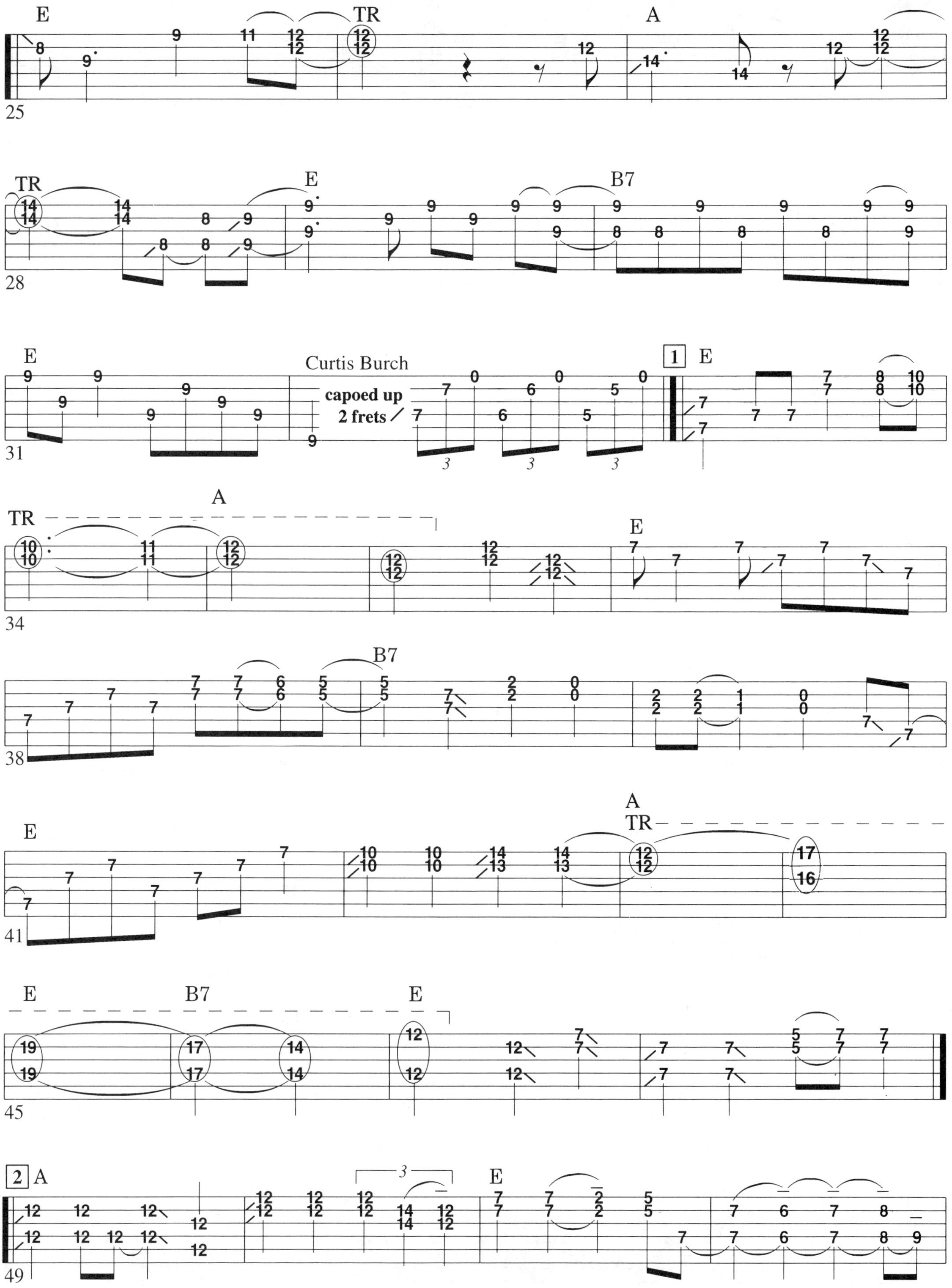
E
TR
A
B7
Curtis Burch
capoed up 2 frets
1
2

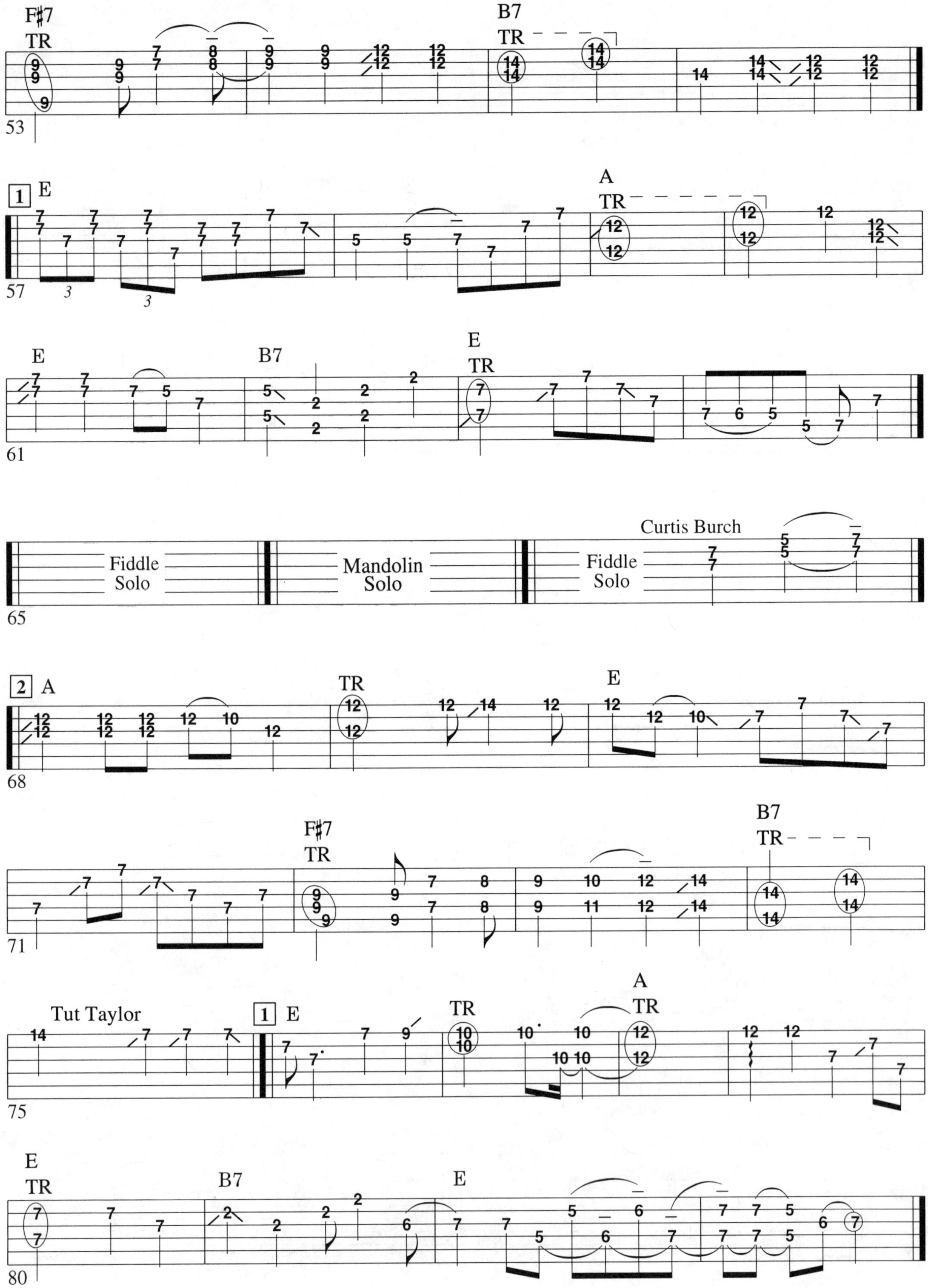
F♯7
B7
E
A
TR
Fiddle Solo
Mandolin Solo
Curtis Burch
Fiddle Solo
Tut Taylor

WAKE FOREST

By **Mike Auldridge**

Mike plays this on his Ivan Guernsey six-string resonator guitar. In the second measure of the introduction the slow slide begins about the third beat. In section one all the D7 chords should begin an eighth note earlier than indicated though it is not obvious in this recording.

In measure 20 the octave on the third fret has no duration. The indicated slide begins immediately. In Mike's second pass at section 1 after the fiddle and banjo solo there is a similar slide. In the measure before the mandolin solo, the double string slide begins almost immediately and takes up the rest of the measure. Mike slides all the way to the nut.

Thanks to Mister Auldridge for revealing the chord progression for me.

Mike Auldridge and Jerry Douglas jamming backstage in 1980. (photo: Carl Fleischauer).

WAKE FOREST

As played by
Mike Auldridge

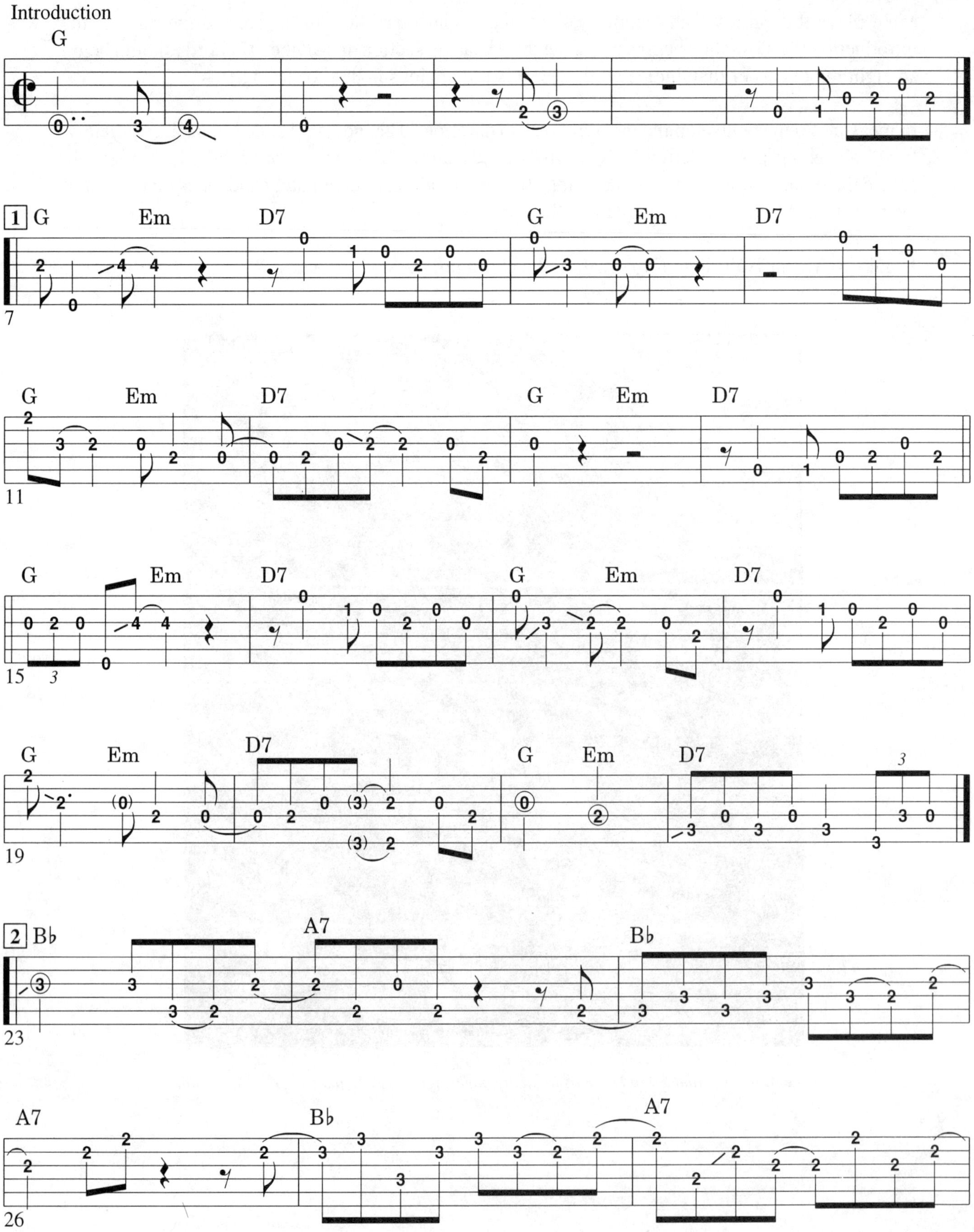

B♭ A7 Am Bm
C D7 Am Bm C D7
Am Bm C D7 Am Bm
C D7
Mandolin Solo
Guitar Solo
Banjo and Fiddle Solo
G Em
D7 G Em D7
G Em D7 G Em D7
G Em D7 G Em D7

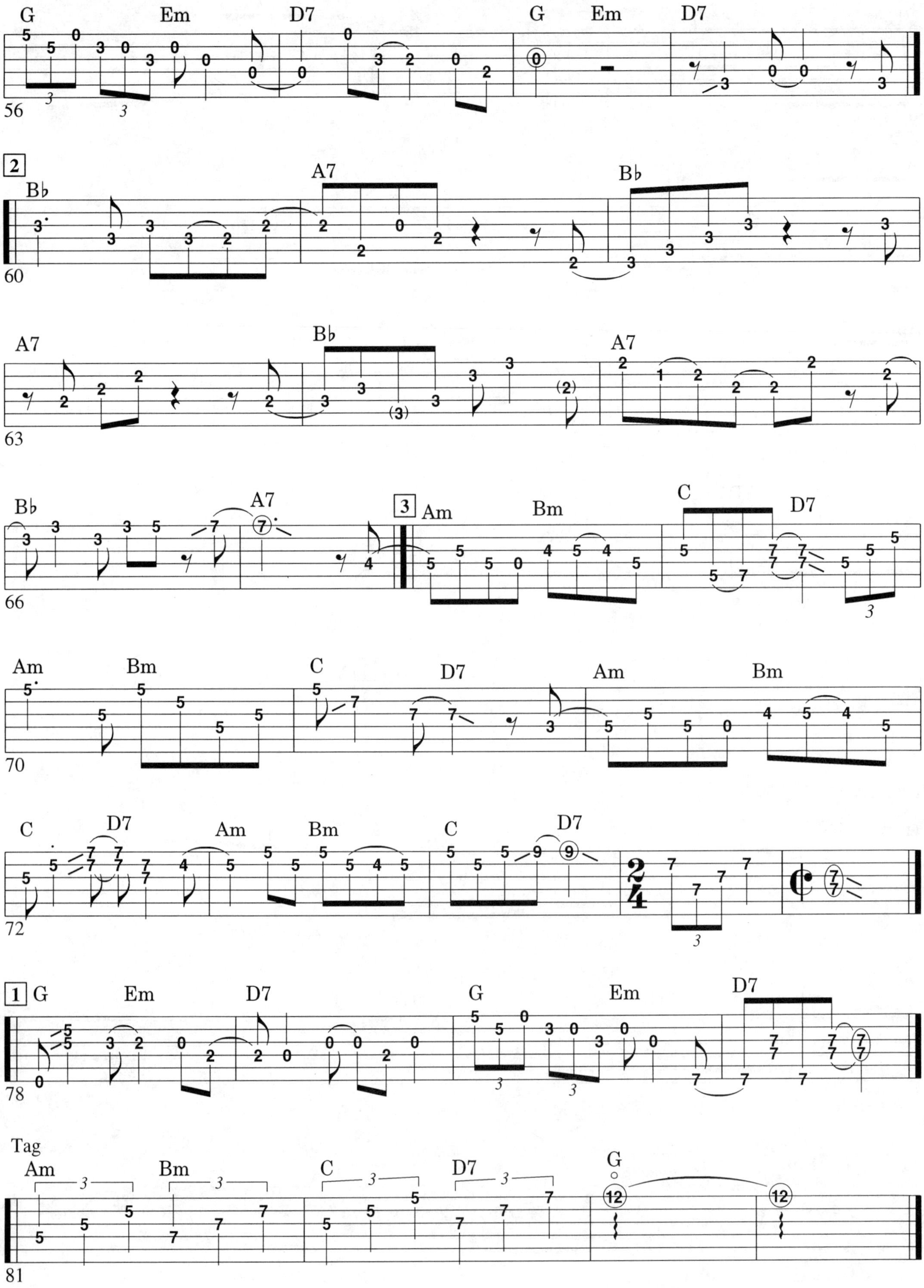
G Em D7 G Em D7
Bb A7 Bb
A7 Bb A7
Bb A7 Am Bm C D7
Am Bm C D7 Am Bm
C D7 Am Bm C D7
G Em D7 G Em D7
Tag
Am Bm C D7 G

THE END OF THE WORLD

By **Fred Rose**

Pete Kirby tunes to an open A chord. Many of the notated double stops are actually phrased as hula picks, i.e. the lower note anticipates as a sort of grace note. It is easier to hear than notate.
The parenthetical notes in measure 19 indicate that the slide starts immediately upon picking.
I could not figure out which strings measures 36-38 were played on. This is my best guess. In measure 40 leave the bar flat and let the notes overlap.

All the tremolos are completely legato and slide-y. Most guitars do not have a 24th fret, so you must rely on scratches on the finish for visual guides, and your ear to find it.

THE END OF THE WORLD

Tuned to A

As played by Pete Kirby

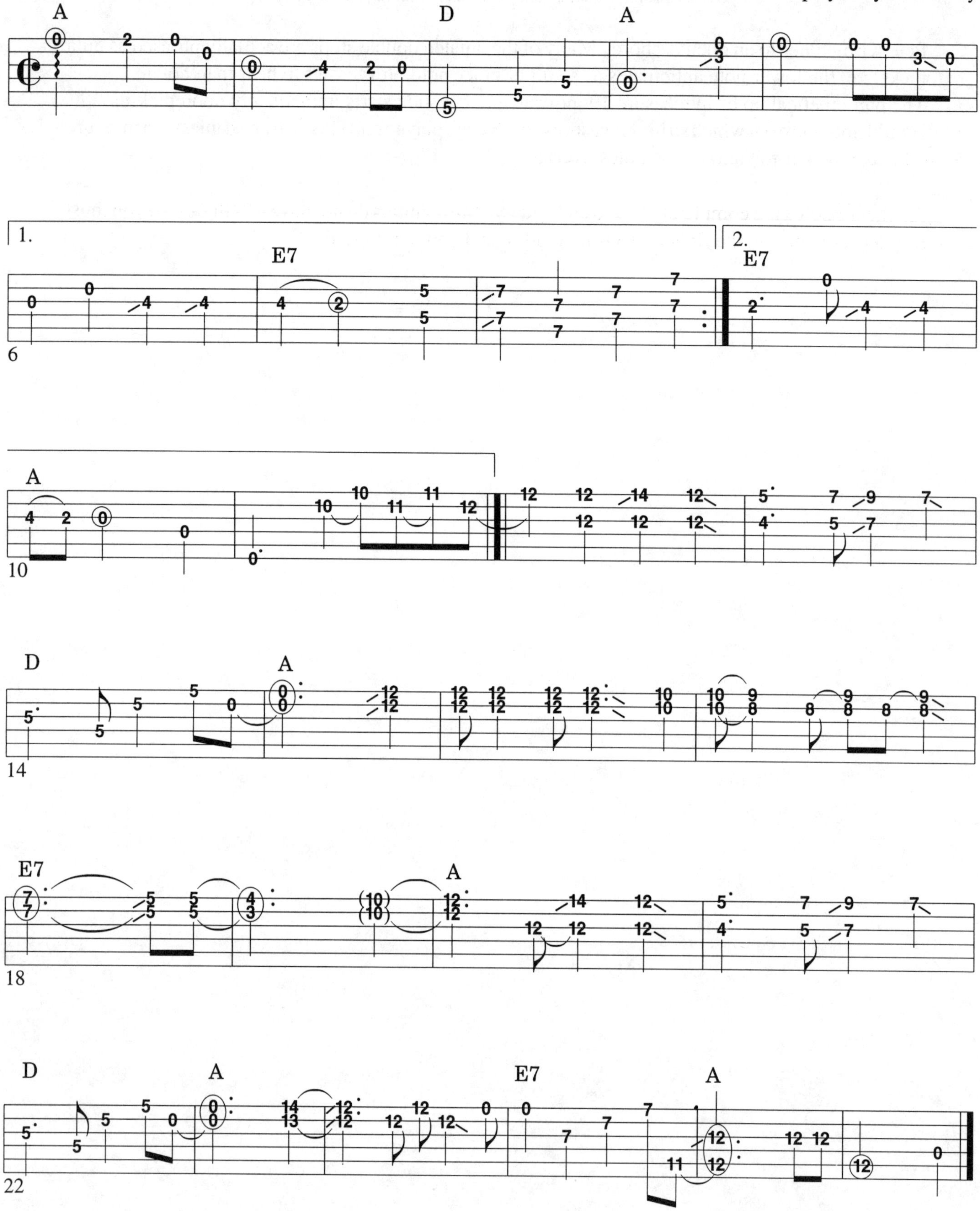

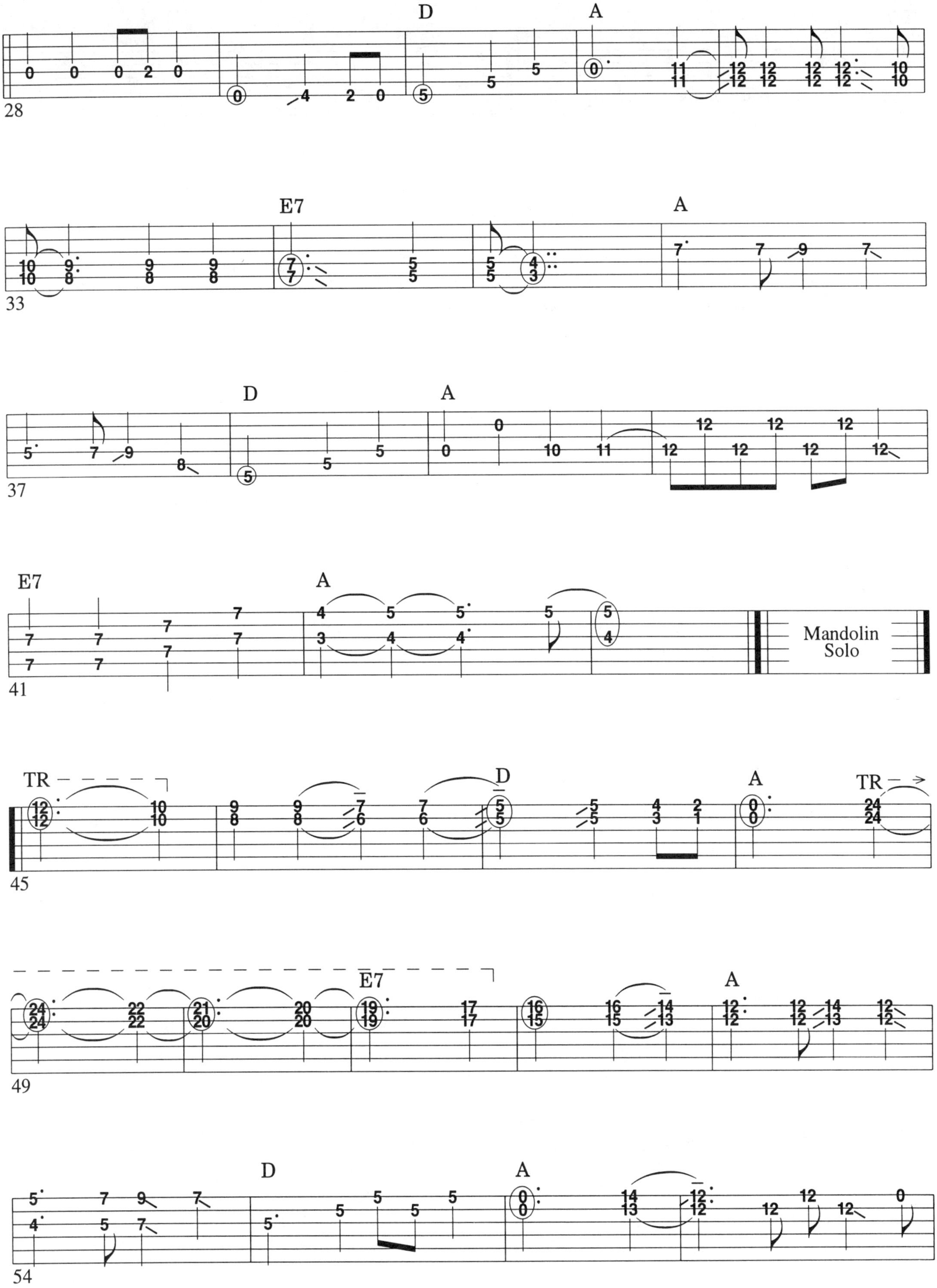
D
A
E7
A
D
A
E7
A
Mandolin
Solo
TR
D
A
TR
E7
A
D
A

E7
A
58
A
E7
64
A
TR
D
68
A
E7
A
72

Other Instructional Material

Contact me through Mel Bay Publications, Inc. (#4 Industrial Drive, Pacific, MO 63069) or at 36 Cromwell Hill Drive, Monroe, NY 10959 for ordering information about these books and tapes.

The Deluxe DOBRO® Tune Book - a giant collection of breakdowns, fiddle tunes, waltzes, rags, and steel guitar classics with plenty of hot licks...expand your musical arsenal with "Arkansas Traveller," "Whistling Rufus," "Home Sweet Home," "John Hardy," "Jaybird," "Dust My Broom," "Down Yonder," "Cuckoo's Nest," "Turkey in the Straw," "Sally Gooden," "Alabama Jubilee," "Ragtime Annie," 80 more... cassette available

The Art of Hawaiian Steel Guitar - over 50 solos with detailed analyses and historical background...solos by Sol Hoopii, Jim and Bob, Jerry Byrd, Benny Nawahi, Sol K. Bright, etc. ... "Maui Chimes," "Moana Chimes," "Song of the Islands," "Hilo March," "Kilima Waltz," "Tomi Tomi," "Tickling the Strings," "Pearly Shells," "Aloha Oe" and 45 more...the only book that tells the whole story...recommended by all the Hawaiian guitar associations, DeWitt Scott (of the steel guitar convention) and Bob Brozman...cassette available

Bluegrass DOBRO® - a six-hour audio cassette course from the basics to advanced hot improvising, with tablature. . ."Columbus Stockade Blues" (four versions), "I'll Be All Smiles Tonight," Oswald-style "Hilo March" and "Great Speckled Bird," Buck Graves-style "Salty Dog Blues" and "Spanish Two Step," "Train 45," bluegrass breakdown licks, "June Apple," "Steel Guitar Rag," "Footprints in the Snow," "Soldier's Joy," "John Henry" and others

Beginning DOBRO® - detailed instruction of elementary techniques. . . designed to fit in your case

The DOBRO® Chord Book- all the chords you will ever need...major, minor, dominant, thirteenths, sixths, etc., plus examples of their use in tunes

The DOBRO® Book - an overview of styles and the great players. . .all the techniques from elementary to advanced are taught with typical solos... "Wabash Cannonball," "Jesse James," "Buck's Stumble," "Fisher's Hornpipe," "Taking Off," "Skin Game Blues," "Oklahoma Stomp," "Steel Guitar Chimes" and many others... solos by Buck Graves, Pete Kirby, Bob Dunn, Joaquin Murphy, etc...recommended by Jerry Douglas, Mike Auldridge, Rob Ickes and many others...the one book you will see in all the top players' music rooms

The Complete DOBRO® Player - This is the new standard in acoustic steel guitar instruction books. . .how to create licks and solos in blues, bluegrass, "sweet" country-folk style, Hawaiian, and swing... 325 detailed examples plus 30 full length solos with analyses...in-depth looks at the styles of and solos by Jerry Douglas, Buck Graves, Mike Auldridge, Bob Dunn, Leon McAuliffe and other greats..."John Henry," "Panhandle Rag," "Tennessee Waltz," "Leather Britches," "Sally Ann," "House of the Rising Sun," "Opus 57," "Dark Hollow," "Don't Let Your Deal Go Down," "Bring It On Down to My House," solos by Shot Jackson, Rob Ickes, Gene Wooten, and many more...the use of easy and effective retunings...interviews with all the top players, music theory for resonator guitarists...fills in the gaps and extends the material of *The DOBRO® Book*...cassette or CD available

Repertoire and Techniques for DOBRO® - two 75 minute videos...#1 features getting into making up your own solos...blues, bluegrass songs and breakdowns... "Little Rosewood Casket," "Trouble in Mind," "Foggy Mountain Rock," "Dixie Hoedown" and "Nine Pound Hammer" (in three keys)...#2 features fiddle tunes, detailed discussion of slants and pulls, and chord/melody solos... "Bill Cheatem," "Cherokee Shuffle," "Kentucky Waltz" and "Last Rose of Autumn"...each accompanied with tablature booklet

Beginning DOBRO® Solos - Easy solos in several styles for beginners...not the same old boring tunes..."Shine On, Harvest Moon," "Saint Louis Blues," "Maui Chimes," "Home Sweet Home," "In the Pines," "Alabama Jubilee," many others...in standard notation and tablature...each tune with complete explanation of rhythm and playing hints...comes with CD

Call 800-996-4455 or write for a free catalog of over 200 folk, bluegrass and acoustic recordings

Great Dobro music on Sugar Hill Records

VARIOUS ARTISTS

SH-2206 **"The Great Dobro Sessions"** (CD / CASS)
GRAMMY winner! It's the "Will the Circle Be Unbroken" project for the dobro, with JERRY DOUGLAS, MIKE AULDRIDGE, CURTIS BURCH, JOSH GRAVES, OSWALD KIRBY, SALLY VAN METER, SAM BUSH, BELA FLECK, and many others. "The range of textures and moods on this 21-track set is unexpectedly diverse; fans of the dobro... will wonder if they have died and gone to heaven." - *Billboard*

MIKE AULDRIDGE

SH-3725 **"Eight String Swing"**
(CD w/ bonus track / CASS)
Bluegrass and swing with the SELDOM SCENE, JIMMY ARNOLD, etc. "Stunning performance." - *Billboard*

SH-3780 **"Treasures Untold"** (CD / CASS)
Superb tribute to the roots of country music, with DOC WATSON, TONY RICE, JOHN STARLING. "A wonderful melange of styles that displays the remarkable musical prowess of world-class players having a great time." - *CMJ*

JERRY DOUGLAS

SH-3797 **"Slide Rule"** (CD / CASS)
With guests ALISON KRAUSS, TIM O'BRIEN, CRAIG SMITH, MAURA O'CONNELL, ALAN O'BRYANT, etc. "The best dobro player on earth has recorded his best album yet..." - *Acoustic Guitar*

SH-3831 **"Under the Wire"** (CD / CASS)
Originally released in 1986 as part of MCA's Master Series, now reissued through Sugar Hill Records due to overwhelming demand! With MARK O'CONNOR, BELA FLECK, SAM BUSH, RUSS BARENBERG, EDGAR MEYER.

SH-3847 **Jerry Douglas & Peter Rowan "Yonder"** (CD / CASS)
Two dynamite performers on one recording! A rich landscape of traditional tunes, originals and favorites from early twentieth century acoustic pickers and singers, including "Lullaby of the Leaves," "Chick-a-li-lee-o," "When You and I Were Young, Maggie," "Wayside Tavern," and more.

JERRY DOUGLAS, RUSS BARENBERG & EDGAR MEYER

SH-3817 **"Skip, Hop & Wobble"** (CD / CASS)
A brilliant acoustic frolic from this superstar trio. "...charged with a feeling of spontaneity and discovery; these players seem to bring out the best in each other."
- *Acoustic Guitar*

SALLY VAN METER

SH-3792 **"All in Good Time"** (CD / CASS)
Amazing dobro release from dobro virtuoso SALLY VAN METER, produced by JERRY DOUGLAS. "Dazzling instrumentals that cross the bluegrass boundary into the acoustic fusion territory of David Grisman and the New Grass Revival."
- *Washington Post*

SUGAR HILL

Available at fine record stores everywhere or by mail order from:

Sugar Hill Records
P.O. Box 55300, Durham, NC 27717-5300
phone 800-996-4455 or 919-489-4349 • fax 919-489-6080